*AIRMONT SHAKESPEARE CLASSICS SERIES*

# Twelfth Night

### By

# 𝕎illiam 𝕊hakespeare

AIRMONT PUBLISHING COMPANY, INC.
22 EAST 60TH STREET · NEW YORK 10022

# PREFACE

For the Airmont series of plays by William Shakespeare, we have chosen a text that we believe more nearly preserves the flavor of the old Shakespearean English than do those of more modernized versions.

In a popular-priced paperback edition, it is almost impossible to include a complete compilation of notes because of the limitations of the format. We suggest that the reader refer to the following excellent textbooks for additional material: The New Valiorum (Cambridge and Arden editions); the Globe edition edited by W. G. Clark and W. A. Wright (1866); the Oxford edition edited by W. J. Craig (1891); and the editions by G. L. Kittredge (1936). Also, the following books will be helpful to a better understanding of Shakespeare: Harley Granville-Barker, *Prefaces to Shakespeare, First Series* (London, 1933); Gerald Sanders, *A Shakespeare Primer* (New York and Toronto, 1945); J. Dover Wilson, *The Essential Shakespeare* (London, 1930; New York, 1932).

Dr. David G. Pitt received his B.A. degree from Mt. Allison University in New Brunswick, and his M.A. and Ph.D. degrees from the University of Toronto. Since 1949, he has been in the English Department of Memorial University of Newfoundland and Professor of English there since 1962. His publications include articles on literary and educational subjects, and editorial work on Shakespeare.

# GENERAL INTRODUCTION

## William Shakespeare: His Life, Times, and Theatre

### HIS LIFE

The world's greatest poet and playwright, often called the greatest Englishman, was born in Stratford-upon-Avon, Warwickshire, in the year 1564. The exact date of his birth is uncertain, but an entry in the Stratford *Parish Register* gives his baptismal date as April 26. Since children were usually baptized two or three days after birth, it is reasonable to assume that he was born on or about April 23—an appropriate day, being the feast of St. George, the patron saint of England.

His father, John Shakespeare, was a glover and dealer in wool and farm products, who had moved to Stratford from Snitterfield, four miles distant, some time before 1552. During his early years in Stratford his business prospered, enabling him to acquire substantial property, including several houses, and to take his place among the more considerable citizens of the town. In 1557 he married Mary, daughter of Robert Arden, a wealthy landowner of Wilmcote, not far from Stratford. Two daughters were born to them before William's birth—Joan, baptized in 1558, and Margaret, baptized in 1562—but both died in infancy. William was thus their third child, though the eldest of those who survived infancy. After him were born Gilbert (1566), another Joan (1569), Anne (1571), Richard (1574), and Edmund (1580).

Very little is positively known (though much is conjectured) about Shakespeare's boyhood and education. We know that for some years after William's birth his father's rise in Stratford society and municipal affairs continued. Many local offices came to him in rapid succession: ale-taster, burgess (a kind of constable), assessor of fines, chamberlain (town treasurer), high bailiff (a kind of magistrate), alderman (town councilor), and chief alderman in 1571. As the son of a man of such eminence in Stratford, Shakespeare undoubtedly attended the local Grammar School. This he was entitled to do free of charge, his father being a town councilor. No records of the school are extant, so that we do not know how good a pupil he was nor what subjects he studied. It is probable that he covered the usual Elizabethan curriculum: an "A B C book," the catechism in Latin and English, Latin grammar, the translation of Latin authors, and perhaps some Greek grammar and translation as well. But family circumstances appear to have curtailed his formal education before it was complete, for shortly before William reached his fourteenth birthday his father's rising fortunes abruptly passed their zenith.

Although we do not know all the facts, it is apparent that about the year 1578, having gone heavily into debt, John Shakespeare lost two large farms inherited by his wife from her father. Thereafter, he was involved in a series of lawsuits, and lost his post on the Stratford town council. Matters got steadily worse for him, until finally, in 1586, he was declared a bankrupt. But by this time the future poet-dramatist was already a family man himself.

In 1582, in the midst of his father's legal and financial crises—and perhaps because of them—Shakespeare married Anne, daughter of Richard Hathaway (recently deceased) of the village of Shottery near Stratford. The *Episcopal Register* for the Diocese of Worcester contains their marriage record, dated November 28, 1582; he was then in his eighteenth year and his wife in her twenty-sixth. On May 26 of the following year the *Stratford Parish Register* recorded the baptism of their first child, Susanna; and on February 2, 1585, the baptism of a twin son and daughter named Hamnet and Judith.

These facts are all that are known of Shakespeare's early life. How he supported his family, whether he took up some trade or profession, how long he continued to live in Stratford, we do not know for certain. Tradition and conjecture have bestowed on him many interim occupations between his marriage and his appearance in London in the early fifteen-nineties: printer, dyer, traveling-player, butcher, soldier, apothecary, thief—it reads like a children's augury-rhyme (when buttons or cherry-stones are read to learn one's fate). Perhaps only the last-named "pursuit" requires some explanation. According to several accounts, one of them appearing in the first *Life* of Shakespeare by Nicholas Rowe (1709), Shakespeare fell into bad company some time after his marriage, and on several occasions stole deer from the park of Sir Thomas Lucy, a substantial gentleman of Charlecote, near Stratford. According to Rowe:

> For this he was prosecuted by that gentleman, as he thought somewhat too severely; and in order to revenge that ill-usage, he made a ballad upon him . . . and was obliged to leave his business and family in Warwickshire, for some time, and shelter himself in London.

The story has been repeated in varying forms by most subsequent biographers, but its authenticity is doubted by many who repeat it.

Another much more attractive story, which, however, if true, does not necessarily deny the authenticity of Rowe's, is that Shakespeare during the so-called "lost years" was a schoolmaster. This, indeed, appears to be somewhat better substantiated. John Aubrey, seventeenth-century biographer and antiquary, in his *Brief Lives* (1681), declares that he had learned from a theatrical manager, whose father had known Shakespeare, that the dramatist "had been in his younger years a schoolmaster in the country." This may, then, account, in part at least, for the years between his marriage and his arrival in London about the year 1591. It is interesting to note that in two of his early plays Shakespeare includes a schoolmaster among his characters: Holofernes of *Love's Labour's Lost* and Pinch of *The Comedy of Errors*. But let us hope that neither is intended to be Shakespeare's portrait of himself!

However he may have occupied himself in the interim, we know that by 1592 he was already a budding actor and play-

wright in London. In that year Robert Greene in his auto-
biographical pamphlet *A Groatsworth of Wit*, referring to
the young actors and menders of old plays who were, it
seemed to him, gaining undeserved glory from the labours of
their betters (both by acting their plays and by rewriting
them), wrote as follows:

> Yes trust them not: for there is an upstart Crow, beauti-
> fied with our feathers, that with his Tygers heart, wrapt
> in a Players hyde, supposes he is as well able to bombast
> out blanke verse as the best of you: and being an ab-
> solute *Johannes factotum*, is in his owne conceit the onely
> Shakescene in a countrey.

"Shakescene" is clearly Shakespeare. The phrase "upstart
Crow" probably refers to his country origins and his lack of
university education. "Beautified with our feathers" probably
means that he uses the older playwrights' words for his own
aggrandisement either in plays in which he acts or in those
he writes himself. "Tygers heart wrapped in a Players hyde" is
a parody of a line in III *Henry VI*, one of the earliest plays
ascribed to Shakespeare. And the Latin phrase *Johannes
factotum*, meaning Jack-of-all-trades, suggests that he was at
this time engaged in all sorts of theatrical jobs: actor, poet,
playwright, and perhaps manager as well.

Greene died shortly after making this scurrilous attack on
the young upstart from Stratford, and so escaped the resent-
ment of those he had insulted. But Henry Chettle, himself
a minor dramatist, who had prepared Greene's manuscript
for the printer, in his *Kind-Harts Dreame* (1592), apologized
to Shakespeare for his share in the offence:

> I am as sory as if the originall fault had beene my fault,
> because my selfe have seene his demeanor no lesse civill,
> than he excelent in the qualitie he professes: Besides, divers
> of worship have reported his uprightnes of dealing, which
> argues honesty, and his facetious grace in writing, that
> approoves his Art.

Thus, in a very indirect manner and because of an attack
upon him by an irascible dying man, we learn that Shakespeare

at this time was in fact held in high regard by "divers of worship," that is, by many of high birth, as an upright, honest young man of pleasant manners and manifest skill as actor, poet, and playwright.

Although Shakespeare by 1593 had written, or written parts of, some five or six plays (I, II, and III *Henry VI*, *Richard III*, *The Comedy of Errors*, and perhaps *Titus Andronicus*), it was as a non-dramatic poet that he first appeared in print. *Venus and Adonis* and *The Rape of Lucrece*, long narrative poems, both bearing Shakespeare's name, were published in 1593 and 1594 respectively. But thereafter for the next twenty years he wrote almost nothing but drama. In his early period, 1591 to 1596, in addition to the plays named above, he wrote *Love's Labour's Lost*, *The Taming of the Shrew*, *Two Gentlemen of Verona*, *Romeo and Juliet*, *A Midsummer Night's Dream*, *Richard II*, and *King John*. Then followed his great middle period, 1596 to 1600, during which he wrote both comedies and history-plays: *The Merchant of Venice*, I and II *Henry IV*, *The Merry Wives of Windsor*, *Much Ado about Nothing*, *Henry V*, *Julius Caesar*, *As You Like It*, and *Twelfth Night*. The period of his great tragedies and the so-called "dark comedies" followed (1600-1608): *Hamlet*, *Troilus and Cressida*, *All's Well that Ends Well*, *Measure for Measure*, *Othello*, *King Lear*, *Macbeth*, *Antony and Cleopatra*, *Timon of Athens*, and *Coriolanus*. The last phase of his career as dramatist, 1608 to 1613, sometimes called "the period of the romances," produced *Pericles, Prince of Tyre*, *Cymbeline*, *The Winter's Tale*, *The Tempest*, parts of *Henry VIII*, and perhaps parts of *The Two Noble Kinsmen*. Many other plays were ascribed to him, but it is doubtful that he had a hand in any but those we have named. Long before his death in 1616 his name held such magic for the public that merely to print it on the title page of any play assured its popular acclaim. The "upstart Crow" had come a long way since 1592.

He had come a long way, too, from the economic straits that may well have driven him to London many years before. We know, for example, from the records of tax assessments that by 1596 Shakespeare was already fairly well-to-do. This is further borne out by his purchasing in the following year a substantial house known as New Place and an acre of land in Stratford for £60, a sizable sum in those days. In 1602 he made a further purchase of 107 acres at Stratford for £320, and a cottage and more land behind his estate at New Place. But his life during this time was not quite unclouded. His only son, Hamnet, died in 1596 at the age of eleven years, his father in 1601, and his mother in 1608. All three were buried in Stratford. More happily he saw, in 1607, the marriage of his daughter Susanna to Dr. John Hall, an eminent physician of Stratford, and, in the following year, the baptism of his granddaughter, Elizabeth Hall.

Shakespeare's retirement to Stratford appears to have been gradual, but by 1613, if not earlier, he seems to have settled there, though he still went up to London occasionally. Of the last months of his life we know little. We do know that in February, 1616, his second daughter, Judith, married Thomas Quiney. We know that on March 25, apparently already ill, Shakespeare revised and signed his will, among other bequests leaving to his wife his "second best bed with the furniture." A month later he was dead, dying on his fifty-second birthday, April 23, 1616. He was buried in the chancel of Holy Trinity Church, Stratford, on April 26.

## HIS TIMES

Shakespeare lived during the English Renaissance, that age of transition that links the Mediaeval and the Modern world. Inheriting the rich traditions of the Middle Ages in art, learning, religion, and politics, rediscovering the great legacies of classical culture, the men of the Renaissance went on to new and magnificent achievements in every phase of human endeavour. No other period in history saw such varied and prolific development and expansion. And the reign of Elizabeth I (1558-1603), Shakespeare's age, was the High Renaissance in England.

Development and expansion—these are the watchwords of the age, and they apply to every aspect of life, thought, and activity. The universe grew in immensity as men gradually abandoned the old Ptolemaic view of a finite, earth-centered universe, accepting the enormous intellectual challenge of the illimitable cosmos of Copernicus' theory and Galileo's telescope. The earth enlarged, too, as more of its surface was discovered and charted by explorers following the lead of Columbus, Cabot, Magellan, and Vespucci. England itself expanded as explorers and colonizers, such as Frobisher, Davis, Gilbert, Raleigh, Grenville, Drake, and others, carried the English flag into many distant lands and seas; as English trade and commerce expanded with the opening of new markets and new sources of supply; as English sea power grew to protect the trading routes and fend off rivals, particularly Spain, the defeat of whose Invincible Armada in 1588 greatly advanced English national pride at home, and power and prestige abroad.

The world of ideas changed and expanded, too. The rediscovery and reinterpretation of the classics, with their broad and humane view of life, gave a new direction and impetus to secular education. During the Middle Ages theology had dominated education, but now the language, literature, and philosophy of the ancient world, the practical arts of grammar, logic, and rhetoric, and training in morals, manners, and gymnastics assumed the major roles in both school and university—in other words, an education that fitted one for life in the world here and now replaced one that looked rather to the life hereafter. Not that the spiritual culture of man was neglected. Indeed, it took on a new significance, for as life in this world acquired new meaning and value, religion assumed new functions, and new vitality to perform them, as the bond between the Creator and a new kind of creation.

It was, of course, the old creation—man and nature—but it was undergoing great changes. Some of these we have already seen, but the greatest was in man's conception of himself and his place in nature. The Mediaeval view of man was generally not an exalted one. It saw him as more or less depraved, fallen from Grace as a result of Adam's sin; and the things of this world, which was also "fallen," as of little value in terms of his salvation. Natural life was thought of mainly as a preparation for man's entry into Eternity. But Renaissance thought soon began to rehabilitate man, nature, and the things of this life. Without denying man's need for Grace and the value of the means of salvation provided by the Church, men came gradually to accept the idea that there were "goods," values, "innocent delights" to be had in the world here and now, and that God had given them for man to enjoy. Man himself was seen no longer as wholly vile and depraved, incapable even of desiring goodness, but rather as Shakespeare saw him in *Hamlet*:

What a piece of work is man! how noble in reason! how infinite in faculty! in form and moving how express and admirable! in action how like an angel! in apprehension how like a god! the beauty of the world! the paragon of animals!

And this is the conception of man that permeates Elizabethan thought and literature. It does not mean that man is incorruptible, immune to moral weakness and folly. Shakespeare has his villains, cowards, and fools. But man is none of these by nature; they are distortions of the true form of man. Nature framed him for greatness, endowed him with vast capacities for knowledge, achievement, and delight, and with aspirations that may take him to the stars. "O brave new world, That has such people in 't!"

The chief object of man's aspiring mind is now the natural world, whose "wondrous architecture," says Marlowe's Tamburlaine, our souls strive ceaselessly to comprehend, "Still climbing after knowledge infinite." Hamlet, too, speaks of "this goodly frame, the earth . . . this brave o'erhanging firmament, this majestical roof fretted with golden fire." No longer the ruins of a fallen paradise and the devil's, nature is seen as man's to possess, her beauty and wonder to be sought after and enjoyed, her energies to be controlled and used—as Bacon expressed it, "for the glory of the Creator and the relief of man's estate."

It was, indeed, a very stirring time to be alive in. New vistas were breaking upon the human mind and imagination everywhere. It was a time like spring, when promise, opportunity, challenge and growth appeared where none had been dreamed of before. Perhaps this is why there is so much poetry of springtime in the age of Shakespeare.

## HIS THEATRE

There were many theatres, or playhouses, in Shakespeare's London. The first was built in 1576 by James Burbage and was called the *Theatre*. It was built like an arena, with a movable platform at one end, and had no seats in the pit, but had benches in the galleries that surrounded it. It was built of wood, and cost about £200. Other famous playhouses of Shakespeare's time, for the most part similarly constructed, included the Curtain, the Bull, the Rose, the Swan, the Fortune, and, most famous of them all, the Globe. It was built in 1599 by the sons of James Burbage, and it was here that most of Shakespeare's plays were performed. Since more is known about the Globe than most of the others, I shall use it as the basis of the brief account that follows of the Elizabethan playhouse.

As its name suggests, the Globe was a circular structure (the second Globe, built in 1614 after the first burned down, was octagonal), and was open to the sky, somewhat like a modern football or baseball stadium, though much smaller. It had three tiers of galleries surrounding the central "yard" or pit, and a narrow roof over the top gallery. But most interesting from our viewpoint was the stage—or rather *stages*—which was very different from that of most modern theatres. These have the familiar "picture-frame" stage: a raised platform at one end of the auditorium, framed by curtains and footlights, and viewed only from the front like a picture. Shakespeare's stage was very different.

The main stage, or *apron* as it was called, jutted well out into the pit, and did not extend all the way across from side to side. There was an area on either side for patrons to sit or stand in, so that actors performing on the apron could be viewed from three sides instead of one. In addition, there was an inner stage, a narrow rectangular recess let into the wall behind the main stage. When not in use it could be closed by a curtain drawn across in front; when open it could be used for interior scenes, arbor scenes, tomb and anteroom scenes and the like. On either side of this inner stage were doors through which the main stage was entered. Besides the inner and outer stages, there were no fewer than four other areas where the action of the play, or parts of it, might be performed. Immediately above the inner stage, and corresponding to it in size and shape, was another room with its front exposed. This was the upper stage, and was used for upstairs scenes, or for storage when not otherwise in use. In front of this was a narrow railed gallery, which could be used for balcony scenes, or ones requiring the walls of a castle or the ramparts of a fortress. On either side of it and on the same level was a window-stage, so-called because it consisted of a small balcony enclosed by windows that opened on hinges. This permitted actors to stand inside and speak from the open windows to others on the main stage below. In all, it was a very versatile multiple stage and gave the dramatist and producer much more freedom in staging than most modern theatres afford. It is interesting to note that some of the new theatres today have revived certain of the features of the Elizabethan stage.

Very little in the way of scenery and backdrops was used. The dramatist's words and the imagination of the audience supplied the lack of scenery. No special lighting effects were possible since plays were performed in the daylight that streamed in through the unroofed top of the three-tiered enclosure that was the playhouse. Usually a few standard stage props were on hand: trestles and boards to form a table, benches and chairs, flagons, an altar, artificial trees, weapons, a man's severed head, and a few other items. Costumes were usually elaborate and gorgeous, though no attempt was made to reproduce the dress of the time and place portrayed in the play.

Play production in Shakespeare's time was clearly very different from that of ours, but we need have no doubts about the audience's response to what they saw and heard on stage. They came, they saw, and the dramatist conquered, for they kept coming back for more and more. And despite the opposition that the theatre encountered from Puritans and others, who thought it the instrument of Satan, the theatre in Shakespeare's time flourished as one of the supreme glories of a glorious age.

—DAVID G. PITT
*Memorial University of Newfoundland*

# INTRODUCTION TO
## *Twelfth Night*

### "THE BEST ENGLISH COMEDY"

No comedy by Shakespeare, or any other English playwright, has been more unreservedly praised than has *Twelfth Night*. William Hazlitt wrote long ago that it is "justly considered as one of the most delightful of Shakespeare's comedies. It is full of sweetness and pleasantry" (*Characters of Shakespeare's Plays*); John Dover Wilson has written of it as the best of Shakespeare's comedies, "which for sheer lightness of touch goes as far as even Shakespeare can reach" (*The Essential Shakespeare*); and John Masefield has called it "the best English comedy" (*Shakespeare*). There are few critics who dissent. It is, indeed, a rare combination of some of the most engaging characters, entertaining situations, charming songs, witty prose, and delightful poetry in the whole world of drama. Above all, it is a superb example of a wide variety of diverse elements fused into a beautifully balanced, carefully controlled artistic whole, which has not only that essential unity of structure, but also a unity of tone and mood that blends and harmonizes the high comedy and the low, the romance and the realism, the light and the shade that the play contains.

The primary elements of which the play is composed run almost the whole gamut of comedy. There is, from romantic comedy, the sentimental, love-sick nobleman and the sentimental, love-sick lady, aloof, proud, disdainful of his love: the love that feeds on music and the love that thrives on grief. There is the situation comedy of love-intrigue, comprising such things as disguise, mistaken identity, a woman loved by another who thinks her a man, and a woman who cannot tell her love. There is the low comedy of the basement kitchen and the wine cellar, with its Falstaffian winebibber and trickster, and his well-matched wench to aid and abet him. There is the comic parody of the courtly lover—cowardly, effeminate, stupid, unheroic, the natural victim of the "guller." There is caricature: of the over-serious man of business, dignified, vain, self-righteous, filled with a sense of his own importance, a caricature of the Puritan, too, who thinks because he is virtuous "there shall be no more cakes and ale." There is comedy such as a clown devises, with his wit and humor, his quaint wisdom and his songs. And there is heroic comedy provided by the brave young stalwart, handsome and energetic, Fortune's darling, who stumbles into luck and love, bringing order out of chaos, and happy resolutions to untoward complications.

Here is variety indeed, so rich as to suggest from a mere catalogue of its items either a very loosely constructed medley of delights, or such a complex concatenation of parts that its carpentry must be all too obvious to the eye. But it is nothing of the sort. Not only is all fused and blended into a perfectly balanced and harmonious whole, but its actual physical construction, its articulation of parts, is beautifully simple. This is not to say that the play lacks complications of plot; a certain amount of complication is essential to any play. But in *Twelfth Night*, as in any well-made play, the complications of plot are not dependent on complexities of structure.

Looking briefly at the skeletal structure of the play, we find, first, a primary situation, in which a man, in love with a woman who refuses to see him, enlists the aid of a girl disguised as a boy to act as his go-between. This simple situation is complicated, first, by the idol of the man's affections falling in love with the disguised emissary, who in turns falls in love with her employer; and, second, by the arrival of an apparent duplicate of the girl-disguised-as-a-boy. To this is added a secondary situation, in which a pair of unlikely suitors for the hand of the lady sought by the man in the first situation are made fools of by two roguish characters, who exist, so far as the plot is concerned, simply to create amusing mischief. The two situations are further linked by one of the suitors being maneuvered into a duel with his supposed rival, the disguised girl of the first situation. The two plots are thus both supplementary and complementary to one another, and are resolved by the same means: the entry of the girl's twin brother, which changes the love triangle of the main plot into a parallelogram, and at the same time thwarts the incongruous intentions of the other two suitors. Thus the brave who deserve the fair get them, and those who deserve nothing get nothing.

Told thus, without the living flesh of dialogue and action, wit and humor, poetry and song upon its bare bones, the play appears perhaps to be a very slight thing. But what is apparent from this divestiture is the nicely balanced, carefully articulated narrative framework of the play that gives it shape and unity. This a good play must have, no matter how fine and proper its other dramatic resources may be. *Twelfth Night* is so good a play, however, because it has everything that a play should have in all the right places. For in addition to its shapely form and outline, it has those fine nuances of light and shade, those contrasts of character and temperament, of mood and feeling, those movements from laughter to sentiment, from absurdity to propriety, from irony to near pathos, that give it variety without disparity, and luxury without luxuriance. Well may it be called "the best English comedy."

## THE THEME OF LOVE

Like the comedies that preceded it, *Twelfth Night* has love as its primary theme. But I think it may be fairly said that in none of the earlier plays has Shakespeare given us a more kindly and sympathetic view of love—be it love "engendered in the eyes," in the heart, or in the head—than we find in this play.

In a sense, he has returned in *Twelfth Night* to the world of "midsummer madness" of *A Midsummer Night's Dream*, but with an important difference: *Twelfth Night* is no world of freakish fairies, magic juices, and heady moonshine. Here it is not the moon-madness of the earlier play. This may be Illyria, as romantically remote as the forest near Athens, but it is Illyria by daylight. And these are not lovers who have

fled the tyranny of parents or of the state, nor are they be-
deviled by fairy sprites. And yet here is Orsino sick with
love, sighing like a furnace, touched in the head. Here is
Viola in love with Orsino, but maintaining a fraud that is
against all reason and sanity, and can only get her into deeper
and deeper trouble. Here is Olivia unreasonably shut up with
her grief, but soon falling in love with a girl dressed up like
a boy. Here is Sir Andrew Aguecheek, mad as a March Hare,
fancying himself in love with a countess. Here is Malvolio,
"sick of self-love," soon to be taken for the madman he
undoubtedly appears to be. Here is Sebastian, sane enough
when he first comes on the scene, soon finding himself at
his wits' end to maintain his sanity, or at least convince himself that he is not mad, so much lunacy seems to be in evidence all around him.

In *A Midsummer Night's Dream* Shakespeare is more than
a little dubious of a passion that links the lover and the
lunatic, and seems to nod approval as Puck exclaims, "Lord,
what fools these mortals be." But in *Twelfth Night* he
seems to have grown more tolerant of the "midsummer madness" of love, and a little less certain that love can be or
ought to be subjected wholly to reason and good sense. In
this play he seems ready to admit that love may, after all,
be a kind of madness, though a divine madness. (Malvolio
and Sir Andrew are, of course, mere parodies of the "pretty
follies" that lovers commit, not to be taken as serious judg-
ments on love.) Love may be a dream, he seems to be saying now, but who wants to awaken from it once one has
known it truly. If Puck sums up, a bit intolerantly perhaps,
one judgment of love, one kind of it or one side of it at least,
Sebastian sums up the later, more kindly, tolerant, even
whimsical, judgment of love in *Twelfth Night*: "If it be thus
to dream, still let me sleep."

Love is seen, in this play at least, as something that cannot be regulated, measured, judged, or even accounted for,
in terms of ordinary rational, clear, cold common sense.
Even at its best and deepest (as is Viola's love for Orsino)
it has about it something of the irrational, incalculable, in-
explicable, even ludicrous and absurd. This is Shakespeare's

most detached judgment on love. Perhaps this is why, after all, *Twelfth Night* is his brightest, gayest, happiest, most carefree play.

## THE CHARACTERS

Viola is the undoubted heroine of the play, and there is no hero. This latter assertion may, perhaps, be wondered at, but if there is a hero who can he possibly be? The sentimental, love-sick duke, who cannot even go to woo the lady he thinks he loves? The fortunate missing brother, who turns up in the nick of time to save his sister and win a wife he did not have to woo? The absurd puritan steward, who fancies himself capable of loving someone other than himself? One or other of the thoroughly unheroic knights? All are quite impossible candidates. To suggest the clown might, perhaps, be no less preposterous. However we may define *hero*—central figure or chief protagonist of the action, the "good" character who wins in the end, the "kingpin" in the structural framework of the play—Viola fulfils all the requirements. She has, moreover, the qualities of character and personality that we look for in a hero: charm, dignity, beauty, integrity, and courage. With her as heroine, the play does not need a hero. One cannot but agree with Hazlitt, who said that the chief reason *Twelfth Night* has always been such a favorite among Shakespeare's plays is the presence in it of Viola. Her disguised confession of love for Orsino, "She never told her love . . ." (Act II, Scene iv) is undoubtedly the emotional center of the play, of which she is the central figure.

Compared with Viola, the Duke is almost a minor character, not so much in the part he plays as in the person he is. He is drawn with neither bold nor vivid strokes. Clearly, Shakespeare intends him to appear thus shadowy, unremarkable, uncharacterized by any particular outstanding quality of intellect or personality. From the opening of the play he is shown as dreamy, imaginative, sentimental, fond of music because he is in love, and in love because he has seen the fair face of an unapproachable lady. Indeed, we get the im-

pression that had Olivia responded to him as she did to the
page he would have shrunk from the encounter. He seems
rather to be in love with love—as an idea, a sentiment. That
he accepts Viola seems due rather to the friendly comrade-
ship that has grown up between them during her masquer-
ade as a boy than to any all-consuming passion for her as
a woman. We may well ask whether he deserves a prize so
estimable. Viola seems to think so, and this in itself must
influence our final estimate of him. It should be remembered,
too, that others speak well of him. The captain calls him,
"A noble duke, in nature as in name," and Olivia, though
she cannot love him, says that she knows him to be noble,
"of fresh and stainless youth;/ In voices well divulged, free,
learn'd and valiant;/ And, in dimension and the shape of
nature,/ A gracious person." I think we can believe that he
and Viola will be happy, for what he lacks in vigor and enter-
prise Viola will make good. Together they should make an
excellent First Lord and Lady in Illyria.

Olivia is in some respects like Orsino—a good reason,
perhaps, for their not marrying each other. Like him, she is
sentimental, rendered "headstrong" by her own emotions.
Thus she lacks the clarity of purpose and intellectual poise
that we see in Viola. Yet she has a certain dignity and charm
of manner, is self-possessed and very able in the management
of her affairs. I think most readers of the play grow fond of
her, because of an undeniable sweetness in her nature. We
feel that her happiness is assured with Sebastian, since he,
resembling Viola, who is very different from Olivia, will
complement her character as Viola will complement the
Duke's.

Though Sebastian's role is not large, I do not think he
can be regarded, as some commentators see him, as a minor
character. He is in fact quite an important one. It is true
that his contributions to the action are largely accidental,
not planned by him or motivated by anything in his own
character. Nevertheless, the whole denouement of the play
depends almost entirely upon him. He is presented to us as
an attractive young fellow, of stalwart and sturdy bearing,
brave, bold, manly, and handsome enough to please the

Lady Olivia. Besides, he is Viola's brother, and this fact, from the moment we first meet him, enhances his virtues in our eyes.

Maria is a very different sort of woman from the others, both in personality and in social background and breeding. She is called Olivia's "gentlewoman," but she spends more time in the company of Sir Toby, Fabian, and the clown than with her mistress. And this says much for the kind of person she is. Her sharp tongue, quick wit, fondness for fun and mischief, make her a worthy member of the noisy company scolded by Malvolio in Act II, Scene iii. It is she, indeed, who after this lively exchange between the revelers and the man she calls "the devil a Puritan," "a time-pleaser," and "an affection'd ass," proposes the "device" by which they will take their revenge. It is she who writes the letter in her mistress's style, drops it where Malvolio will find it, and generally conducts the whole plot that so successfully traps the vain and pompous steward. Her role in the play is thus one of great importance, and the focal point of much of the best comedy.

Along with Maria, Sir Toby Belch and Sir Andrew Aguecheek provide most of the "low" comedy in the play. While Shakespeare drew many of the story elements from various sources, and while many of his characters had their pale originals in other works, Sir Toby and Sir Andrew are entirely new creations. Their thoroughly English names, a little out of place perhaps among the Italian names of the others, remind us of their English comic background, as well as the great difference between their roles and those of the other characters. Their names suggest much about their natures, and they are as different as their names suggest. Sir Toby is boisterous and jovial, full of wit and humor, fond of the bottle and of food, portly of figure, florid of face, loud and booming of voice. Sir Andrew is almost the opposite of this, except for his fondness for drink. He is timid and cowardly, lacking in wit, and capable of only the feeblest humor. He is lean and pale, with flaxen hair and a "cracked treble voice," more like an old woman than a manly knight. Shakespeare seems to have intended them to balance each other off, and this they effectively do.

This brings us to the object of Maria's and Sir Toby's machinations and the central figure in the subplot of *Twelfth Night*: Malvolio. Having made a number of observations about Malvolio's personality and character already, I shall not repeat them here. But there is still the troubling question: How did Shakespeare really intend him to be understood and interpreted? There are some critics who believe that he is intended, simply, to be a ridiculous, conceited, affected simpleton, the proper butt of all the practical jokes that expose him for what he really is. According to this view, he richly deserves to be made the egregious object of all the sport his tormentors can devise, and his parting words, "I'll be revenged on the whole pack of you," are intended as the helpless boast of an ineffectual fool. But other readers take a different view. They point to his good qualities: his business acumen, his loyalty to his employer, his conscientiousness, earnestness, and dignified bearing. In particular, they find it hard to see the full humor of the "dark-room" scene. According to this more charitable view, Malvolio is indeed "notoriously abused," and while his absurd and excessive self-esteem, his total lack of all sense of humor, his stiffness, his gullibility, all deserve to be chastened, the treatment he actually receives is out of all proportion to his deserts. Thus, in the end he becomes an almost pathetic figure who is out of place in pure comedy. Both of these are extreme views, and the truth probably lies somewhere in between. My own view is that if skilfully played, with just the right touch of absurdity, the role can be a highly amusing one. Absurd rather than contemptible, comic rather than pathetic is, I think, what Shakespeare intended.

There remains only Feste, the Clown, to complete our brief study of the main characters. By "clown" is meant, of course, not what we usually mean by the word, but rather "waggish fellow," "wit," or "funnyman." The type was a great favorite with Elizabethan audiences, for he helped to spice up the action with wit and humor, songs and dances, and sometimes played a significant part in the action. Feste is one of Shakespeare's best, his songs in particular being among the most memorable in the whole of comedy.

The play ends, when all the threads are tied up, with a

song by Feste, the well-known, "When that I was . . . a little tiny boy." It makes a very appropriate epilogue for such a play as *Twelfth Night*. It traces the course of a man's life from childhood through manhood, marriage, and old age. It thus presents a picture of life, not in a serious or profoundly philosophical manner, but rather in a lighthearted and whimsical humor, with just a touch of irony in the refrain, "For the rain it raineth every day." This is just the kind of picture given in the play, of human life as a mixture of many things, none of which is portrayed in its deeper hues, but rather in those that belong to comedy, which ought to be lighthearted, with just a touch of gentle irony. The song is thus a little summary if not of the narrative theme of the play, then of its mood and spirit—a fitting close to a tale that has been full of good fun, and ended happily.

—DAVID G. PITT,
*Professor of English*
*Memorial University of Newfoundland*

# STUDY QUESTIONS

## ACT I

1. The first act of a play is usually called the *exposition*. Its function is to inform us of what we need to know in order to understand and appreciate what is to follow, to introduce some of the characters, to establish the mood and atmosphere of the play, and get the action off to a good start. Discuss the first act of *Twelfth Night* as exposition.

2. What are your first impressions of the Duke, and of Viola?

3. Describe briefly the general atmosphere of Scene iii. How is it created? In what ways does it contrast with the two preceding scenes?

4. What hints are dropped in Scene ii that Sebastian may yet be alive? What is the dramatic value of these hints?

5. How are the characters of Sir Toby, Sir Andrew, and Maria suggested by the language that they use?

6. Is there any irony in Shakespeare's initial portrait of Sir Andrew in Scene iii, both in the references to him before he appears and in the picture he presents of himself when he does? Discuss.

7. What future complication is forecast in Scene iv? How?

8. "The wit of the Clown is well-matched with that of Maria." Do you agree? Defend your answer, using illustrations from Scene v.

9. Scene v is an important and crucial scene. List briefly its main contributions to the development of the plot.

10. What are your initial impressions of Olivia and Malvolio? How are these impressions conveyed? Give illustrations.

11. Are we prepared for Olivia's infatuation with Cesario? Discuss.

## ACT II

1. What are your first impressions of Sebastian? To what extent might one reading or seeing the play for the first time be led to guess certain implications of his arrival in Illyria?

2. Consider Viola's soliloquy beginning, "I left no ring with her."
   (a) What new light does it throw on Viola's nature?
   (b) How does it point up the significance of the new complication created by Olivia's falling in love with the page?
   (c) Comment on its poetry.

3. Briefly describe, as it might be shown on stage, the scene that Malvolio bursts in upon in Scene iii. Do you feel that his scolding has any justification? Discuss.

4. "Sir Toby's rhetorical question addressed to Malvolio, 'Dost thou think, because thou art virtuous, there shall be no more cakes and ale?' epitomizes the character of both." Discuss.

5. What reasons does Maria give for her plan of revenge on Malvolio? Do they seem valid ones at this point in the play? Why? What is her plan?

6. How do Curio's music and Feste's song help to create the right atmosphere for Scene iv, especially its second half?

7. What justification is there for calling Viola's speech to Orsino, beginning, "A blank, my Lord. She never told her love . . ." the "emotional center of the play"?

8. What prior evidence have we of Malvolio's character to make us believe that he will fall into the trap that has been laid for him?

9. What are the main sources of interest and humor in Scene v?

10. Summarize the new developments in the action contributed by Act II.

## ACT III

1. Compare Viola's exchanges with the Clown at the beginning of Scene i with Olivia's dialogue with him in Act I, Scene v. What differences in temperament and sense of humor between the two women are thereby revealed? In what ways is the Clown consistent in his wit?

2. How does Shakespeare use poetry to reinforce the dramatic effects of the encounter between Viola and Olivia in Scene i?

3. What new plot is hatched in Scene ii? How does Sir Toby's part in it reveal his real attitude toward Sir Andrew?

4. How does Scene iii lay the groundwork for future developments?

5. Scene v is a long one and falls into several fairly distinct parts. Indicate each of these and give it an identifying title. Show how each part contributes to the development of the action.

6. What further light does Scene iv shed on the character of each of the following: Olivia, Malvolio, Sir Andrew, Sir Toby?

7. Several distinct types of humor occur in Scene iv. Give examples of each, and try to label or otherwise identify each type.

8. Outline briefly the new developments in this act of (a) the main plot, (b) the subplot, and show how they have come to be more closely linked to one another.

## ACT IV

1. On what basic situation does the humor of Scene i depend? How does Shakespeare make the most of it? Is it effective? Why?

2. Readers and critics have responded differently to Scene ii. Some find its humor "labored and heavy-handed";

others feel that it fails as comedy because in it Malvolio becomes a "pathetic figure"; still others find it "pure comedy" throughout. Comment on each of these views, indicating which one you are in most agreement with, and why.

3. What new and, perhaps, unsuspected qualities of character does Malvolio reveal in Scene ii?

4. Is your opinion of the Clown changed as a result of his behavior in Scene ii? Defend your answer.

5. "Malvolio in the dark room protesting his sanity is a kind of parody in anticipation of Sebastian in the sunlit garden virtually protesting his madness." Discuss.

6. Do you feel that the betrothal of Sebastian and Olivia is adequately prepared for? What new complications does it portend?

## ACT V

1. This act consists of a single long scene. Briefly trace the stages by which the action of the scene develops. What do you consider the real climax of the scene? Why?

2. Do you find at all improbable (a) the Duke's ready acceptance of Viola's love once her identity is known, (b) Olivia's acceptance of Sebastian when he is revealed as Cesario's brother, (c) the news that Sir Toby and Maria have married? Give reasons for your answer in each case.

3. Describe how you think the part of Malvolio should be played in this scene.

4. Imagine a scene preceding this one, in which we are shown Sebastian, anxious to escape matrimony, setting sail from Illyria with Antonio, who has escaped from his captors. Write, as a prose summary, an alternative ending based on this supposition. Do you think that a satisfying denouement could be made without Sebastian's presence?

5. "At the end of the play Orsino has Viola, Olivia has Sebastian, Sir Toby has Maria; even Malvolio has a grievance to cherish and the belated pity of Olivia. Of

the main characters only Sir Andrew gets nothing—
except 'a bloody coxcomb.' " Do you think this a fitting
disposal of Sir Andrew? Why?

6. Why do you think that the Clown's song at the end is
usually considered a most fitting conclusion for this play?

## General Questions

1. Discuss *Twelfth Night* as popular entertainment, paying
particular attention to the methods and devices used to
arouse and maintain the interest of the audience.

2. From your knowledge of the Globe Theatre (see Introduction) describe how any three scenes in the play might
have been presented there.

3. Read the section entitled "The Theme of Love" in the
Introduction to this play, and *either* defend *or* reject
the thesis outlined there respecting Shakespeare's attitude
toward love in this play. Illustrate your answer from the
text of the play.

4. Write briefly on (a) comedy of character, and (b) comedy of situation in this play.

5. Show how music and song are used in *Twelfth Night* to
create the right atmosphere for a play of this kind.

6. Which one of the comic characters of the subplot do you
find most entertaining, and which one least entertaining?
Give reasons in both cases.

7. Some critics say that the so-called subplot in *Twelfth
Night* is too closely interwoven with the main plot to be
properly called a subplot at all. Do you agree? Defend
your answer.

8. "*Twelfth Night* is above all a play of sentiment and
feeling rather than of ideas and intellect." Do you agree?
Defend your answer.

9. "This play has moments that come close to pathos if
not to the full emotions of tragedy." Do you agree.
Discuss.

10. Give your final estimate of the character of each of
Orsino, Viola, Olivia, Malvolio, and Maria.

11. Write an essay on one or more of the following in *Twelfth Night:*

    (a) imagery and figura-      (d) irony
        tive language            (e) satire
    (b) verbal humor             (f) the role of chance
    (c) the use of contrast

12. Identify each of the following passages by speaker and occasion, state its meaning, and its bearing, if any, on the dramatic action, and indicate what light it may shed on the character of the speaker:

    (a)                                         Diana's lip
        Is not more smooth and rubious; thy small pipe
        Is as the maiden's organ, shrill and sound;
        And all is semblative a woman's part.

    (b) Love make his heart of flint, that you shall love;
        And let your fervour, like my master's, be
        Placed in contempt! Farewell, fair cruelty.

    (c) Mistress Mary, if you prized my lady's favour at any thing more than contempt, you would not give means for this uncivil rule: she shall know of it, by this hand.

    (d) The clock upbraids me with the waste of time.—
        Be not afraid, good youth, I will not have you;
        And yet, when wit and youth is come to harvest,
        Your wife is like to reap a proper man.

    (e) He is a knight, dubb'd with unhatched rapier and on carpet consideration; but he is a devil in private brawl: souls and bodies hath he divorced three; and his incensement at this moment is so implacable that satisfaction can be none but by pangs of death and sepulchre.

    (f) For though my soul disputes well with my sense,
        That this may be some error, but no madness,
        Yet doth this accident and flood of fortune
        So far exceed all instance, all discourse,
        That I am ready to distrust mine eyes . . .

# TWELFTH NIGHT; OR, WHAT YOU WILL

## DRAMATIS PERSONAE

ORSINO, *Duke of Illyria.*
SEBASTIAN, *a young gentleman.*
ANTONIO, *a sea captain, friend to Sebastian.*
A SEA CAPTAIN, *friend to Viola.*
VALENTINE,
CURIO, } *gentlemen attending on the Duke.*
SIR TOBY BELCH, *uncle to Olivia.*
SIR ANDREW AGUECHEEK.
MALVOLIO, *steward to Olivia.*
FABIAN,
CLOWN, } *servants to Olivia.*
OLIVIA.
VIOLA, *sister to Sebastian.*
MARIA, *Olivia's woman.*
LORDS, *a* PRIEST, SAILORS, OFFICERS,
MUSICIANS, *and* ATTENDANTS.

SCENE—*A city in Illyria, and the sea-coast near it.*

# Twelfth Night

## ACT 1

# ACT I

Orsino, Duke of Illyria, is in love with the Countess Olivia, who, because her brother has recently died, has shut herself up and refuses to receive any communication from would-be suitors. Now it so happens that a young lady, Viola, is cast ashore from a shipwreck on the coast of Illyria, believing her brother Sebastian to have been drowned. For safety's sake she disguises herself as a young man, Cesario, and makes her way to the Duke's court, where she is taken into his service as a page. Before long, Orsino sends her to Olivia to woo her in his behalf. This is very ironic, for Viola herself has already fallen in love with the Duke. At the Countess's house is a group of riotous fun-loving and fun-making people: Maria, the chamberwoman; Sir Toby Belch, Olivia's uncle; Sir Andrew Aguecheek, a foolish knight who hopes to win Olivia's hand; and Feste, the clown or jester. Also in the household, though very different in temperament from the others, is Malvolio, Olivia's steward, a self-opinionated, haughty fellow. Into this ménage Viola comes (as the page Cesario), and conveys the Duke's message of love to Olivia. Olivia will have none of it and sends Viola away, but not before she has fallen in love with the young page. Thus, by the time the act ends, a curious love triangle has appeared: Orsino in love with Olivia, Olivia in love with Viola (Cesario), and Viola in love with Orsino.

# ACT I. SCENE I.

### The DUKE's palace.

*Enter* DUKE, LORDS, *and* CURIO; MUSICIANS *attending.*

DUKE OF ILLYRIA.

If music be the food of love, play on;
Give me excess of it, that, surfeiting,
The appetite may sicken, and so die.—
That strain again!—it had a dying fall:[1]
O, it came o'er my ear like the sweet sound,
That breathes upon a bank of violets,
Stealing and giving odour!—Enough; no more;
'Tis not so sweet now as it was before.
O spirit of love, how quick and fresh art thou!
That, notwithstanding thy capacity
Receiveth as the sea, naught enters there,
Of what validity and pitch[2] soe'er,
But falls into abatement[3] and low price,
Even in a minute! so full of shapes is fancy,
That it alone is high-fantastical.[4]

---

[1] fall: beat; cadence.
[2] validity and pitch: value.
[3] abatement: lessening in value.
[4] high-fantastical: highly imaginative.

CURIO.

Will you go hunt, my lord?

DUKE OF ILLYRIA.

What, Curio?

CURIO.

The hart.[1]

DUKE OF ILLYRIA.

Why, so I do, the noblest that I have:
O, when mine eyes did see Olivia first,
Methought she purged the air of pestilence!
That instant was I turn'd into a hart;
And my desires, like fell [2] and cruel hounds,
E'er since pursue me.

*Enter* VALENTINE.

How now! what news from her?

VALENTINE.

So please my lord, I might not be admitted;
But from her handmaid do return this answer:
The element[3] itself, till seven years hence,
Shall not behold her face at ample view;
But, like a cloistress,[4] she will veiled walk,
And water once a day her chamber round
With eye-offending brine: all this to season
A brother's dead love,[5] which she would keep fresh
And lasting in her sad remembrance.

DUKE OF ILLYRIA.

O, she that hath a heart of that fine frame
To pay this debt of love but to a brother,
How will she love, when the rich golden shaft[6]
Hath kill'd the flock of all affections else
That live in her; when liver, brain, and heart,
These sovereign thrones, are all supplied, and fill'd

---

[1] hart: a stag; male deer: pun on heart. [2] fell: destructive. [3] element: the world around us. [4] cloistress: a nun. [5] With eye-offending brine; all this to season/ A brother's dead love: to preserve with tears her brother's memory. [6] golden shaft: Cupid's dart.

Her sweet perfections with one self king! [1]—
Away before me to sweet beds of flowers:
Love-thoughts lie rich when canopied with bowers. [*Exeunt.*

## SCENE II.

### *The sea-coast.*

#### *Enter* VIOLA, CAPTAIN, *and* SAILORS.

VIOLA.
What country, friends, is this?
CAPTAIN.
This is Illyria, lady.
VIOLA.
And what should I do in Illyria?
My brother he is in Elysium.[2]
Perchance he is not drown'd:—what think you, sailors?
CAPTAIN.
It is perchance that you yourself were saved.
VIOLA.
O my poor brother! and so perchance may he be.
CAPTAIN.
True, madam; and, to comfort you with chance,
Assure yourself, after our ship did split,
When you, and those poor number saved with you,
Hung on our driving boat,[3] I saw your brother,
Most provident in peril, bind himself—
Courage and hope both teaching him the practice—
To a strong mast that lived upon the sea;
Where, like Arion[4] on the dolphin's back,
I saw him hold acquaintance with the waves[5]
So long as I could see.

---

[1] one self king: one man above all. [2] Elysium: Heaven; the abode of happy souls after death. [3] driving boat: storm-tossed. [4] Arion: a Greek poet who escaped from murderous sailors by riding on a dolphin. [5] hold acquaintance with the waves: keep afloat; stay on top of the water.

VIOLA.

For saying so, there's gold:
Mine own escape unfoldeth to my hope,
Whereto thy speech serves for authority,[1]
The like of him. Know'st thou this country?

CAPTAIN.

Ay, madam, well; for I was bred and born
Not three hours' travel from this very place.

VIOLA.

Who governs here?

CAPTAIN.

A noble duke, in nature as in name.

VIOLA.

What is his name?

CAPTAIN.

Orsino.

VIOLA.

Orsino! I have heard my father name him:
He was a bachelor then.

CAPTAIN.

And so is now, or was so very late;[2]
For but a month ago I went from hence,
And then 'twas fresh in murmur,[3]—as, you know,
What great ones do, the less will prattle of,—
That he did seek the love of fair Olivia.

VIOLA.

What's she?

CAPTAIN.

A virtuous maid, the daughter of a count
That died some twelvemonth since; then leaving her
In the protection of his son, her brother,
Who shortly also died: for whose dear loss,
They say, she hath abjured the company

---

[1] **Mine own escape unfoldeth to my hope,/ Whereto thy speech serves for authority,:** the fact of her escape and his words give hope for her brother's survival.

[2] **late:** lately; recently.

[3] **fresh in murmur:** new gossip.

And sight of men.

    VIOLA.

             O, that I served that lady,
And might not be deliver'd to the world,
Till I had made mine own occasion mellow,
What my estate is!

    CAPTAIN.

             That were hard to compass;[1]
Because she will admit no kind of suit,
No, not the duke's.

    VIOLA.

There is a fair behaviour in thee, captain;
And though that nature with a beauteous wall
Doth oft close in pollution, yet of thee
I will believe thou hast a mind that suits
With this thy fair and outward character.
I prithee,—and I'll pay thee bounteously,—
Conceal me what I am; and be my aid
For such disguise as haply shall become
The form of my intent. I'll serve this duke:
Thou shalt present me as an eunuch[2] to him:
It may be worth thy pains; for I can sing,
And speak to him in many sorts of music,
That will allow me very worth his service.
What else may hap, to time I will commit;
Only shape thou thy silence to my wit.[3]

    CAPTAIN.

Be you his eunuch, and your mute I'll be:
When my tongue blabs, then let mine eyes not see.

    VIOLA.

I thank thee: lead me on.               [*Exeunt.*

---

[1] compass: to bring about.

[2] eunuch: a castrated male.

[3] shape thou thy silence to my wit: keep quiet about her planned disguise.

## SCENE III.

### OLIVIA's house.

*Enter* SIR TOBY BELCH *and* MARIA.

SIR TOBY BELCH.

What a plague means my niece, to take the death of her brother thus? I am sure care's an enemy to life.

MARIA.

By my troth, Sir Toby, you must come in earlier o'nights: your cousin, my lady, takes great exceptions to your ill hours.

SIR TOBY BELCH.

Why, let her except before excepted.[1]

MARIA.

Ay, but you must confine[2] yourself within the modest limits of order.

SIR TOBY BELCH.

Confine! I'll confine myself no finer than I am: these clothes are good enough to drink in; and so be these boots too,—an they be not, let them hang themselves in their own straps.

MARIA.

That quaffing and drinking will undo you: I heard my lady talk of it yesterday; and of a foolish knight that you brought in one night here to be her wooer.

SIR TOBY BELCH.

Who, Sir Andrew Aguecheek?

MARIA.

Ay, he.

SIR TOBY BELCH.

He's as tall [3] a man as any's in Illyria.

---

[1] except before excepted: reference to and a play on a law term (taking exception); Sir Toby intends to do as he pleases.
[2] confine: clothe.
[3] tall: upstanding; courageous.

MARIA.

What's that to th'purpose?

SIR TOBY BELCH.

Why, he has three thousand ducats a year.

MARIA.

Ay, but he'll have but a year in all these ducats: he's a very fool and a prodigal.

SIR TOBY BELCH.

Fie, that you'll say so! he plays o'th'viol-de-gamboys,[1] and speaks three or four languages word for word without book, and hath all the good gifts of nature.

MARIA.

He hath, indeed, almost natural:[2] for, besides that he's a fool, he's a great quarreller; and, but that he hath the gift of a coward to allay the gust he hath in quarrelling, 'tis thought among the prudent he would quickly have the gift of a grave.

SIR TOBY BELCH.

By this hand, they are scoundrels and substractors[3] that say so of him. Who are they?

MARIA.

They that add, moreover, he's drunk nightly in your company.

SIR TOBY BELCH.

With drinking healths to my niece: I'll drink to her as long as there is a passage in my throat and drink in Illyria: he's a coward and a coistrel [4] that will not drink to my niece till his brains turn o'th'toe like a parish-top. What, wench! *Castiliano volto;*[5] for here comes Sir Andrew Agueface.[6]

---

[1] viol-de-gamboys: a musical instrument.
[2] natural: a simpleton.
[3] substractors: detractors.
[4] coistrel: a stable hand: mean, despicable fellow.
[5] *Castiliano volto:* an indeterminate phrase or oath.
[6] Agueface: nickname; a pun on the name Aguecheek.

*Enter* SIR ANDREW AGUECHEEK.

SIR ANDREW AGUECHEEK.

Sir Toby Belch,—how now, Sir Toby Belch!

SIR TOBY BELCH.

Sweet Sir Andrew!

SIR ANDREW AGUECHEEK.

Bless you, fair shrew.

MARIA.

And you too, sir.

SIR TOBY BELCH.

Accost, Sir Andrew, accost.

SIR ANDREW AGUECHEEK.

What's that?

SIR TOBY BELCH.

My niece's chambermaid.

SIR ANDREW AGUECHEEK.

Good Mistress Accost, I desire better acquaintance.

MARIA.

My name is Mary, sir.

SIR ANDREW AGUECHEEK.

Good Mistress Mary Accost,—

SIR TOBY BELCH.

You mistake, knight: 'accost' is front her, board her, woo her, assail her.

SIR ANDREW AGUECHEEK.

By my troth, I would not undertake her in this company. Is that the meaning of 'accost'?

MARIA.

Fare you well, gentlemen.

SIR TOBY BELCH.

An thou let part so, Sir Andrew, would thou mightst never draw sword again.

SIR ANDREW AGUECHEEK.

An you part so, mistress, I would I might never draw sword
again. Fair lady, do you think you have fools in hand?

MARIA.

Sir, I have not you by th'hand.

SIR ANDREW AGUECHEEK.

Marry,[1] but you shall have; and here's my hand.

MARIA.

Now, sir, thought is free: I pray you, bring your hand to
th'buttery-bar,[2] and let it drink.

SIR ANDREW AGUECHEEK.

Wherefore, sweet-heart? what's your metaphor?

MARIA.

It's dry, sir.

SIR ANDREW AGUECHEEK.

Why, I think so: I am not such an ass but I can keep my
hand dry. But what's your jest?

MARIA.

A dry jest, sir.

SIR ANDREW AGUECHEEK.

Are you full of them?

MARIA.

Ay, sir, I have them at my fingers' ends: marry, now I let go
your hand, I am barren.[3]                              [*Exit.*

SIR TOBY BELCH.

O knight, thou lack'st a cup of canary:[4] when did I see thee
so put down?

SIR ANDREW AGUECHEEK.

Never in your life, I think; unless you see canary put me
down. Methinks sometimes I have no more wit than a Chris-

---

[1] **Marry:** an oath; short for "by the Virgin Mary."
[2] **buttery-bar:** mixing bar.
[3] **barren:** lacking any more words to say.
[4] **canary:** wine of the Canary Islands.

tian or an ordinary man has: but I am a great eater of beef,
and I believe that does harm to my wit.[1]

SIR TOBY BELCH.

No question.

SIR ANDREW AGUECHEEK.

An I thought that, I'ld forswear it. I'll ride home to-morrow,
Sir Toby.

SIR TOBY BELCH.

*Pourquoi*, my dear knight?

SIR ANDREW AGUECHEEK.

What is *pourquoi?* do or not do? I would I had bestow'd
that time in the tongues that I have in fencing, dancing, and
bear-baiting: O, had I but follow'd the arts!

SIR TOBY BELCH.

Then hadst thou had an excellent head of hair.

SIR ANDREW AGUECHEEK.

Why, would that have mended my hair?

SIR TOBY BELCH.

Past question; for thou seest it will not curl by nature.

SIR ANDREW AGUECHEEK.

But it becomes me well enough, does't not?

SIR TOBY BELCH.

Excellent; it hangs like flax on a distaff; and I hope to see a
housewife take thee between her legs and spin it off.

SIR ANDREW AGUECHEEK.

Faith, I'll home to-morrow, Sir Toby: your niece will not be
seen; or if she be, it's four to one she'll none of me: the
count himself here hard by[2] woos her.

---

[1] eater of beef,/ and I believe that does harm to my wit: common
belief of the day; i.e., fish was considered a brain food.
[2] hard by: nearby.

SIR TOBY BELCH.

She'll none o'th'count: she'll not match above her degree, neither in estate, years, nor wit; I have heard her swear't. Tut, there's life in't,[1] man.

SIR ANDREW AGUECHEEK.

I'll stay a month longer. I am a fellow o'th' strangest mind i'th'world; I delight in masks and revels sometimes altogether.

SIR TOBY BELCH.

Art thou good at these kickshawses,[2] knight?

SIR ANDREW AGUECHEEK.

As any man in Illyria, whatsoever he be, under the degree of my betters; and yet I will not compare with a nobleman.

SIR TOBY BELCH.

What is thy excellence in a galliard,[3] knight?

SIR ANDREW AGUECHEEK.

Faith, I can cut a caper.

SIR TOBY BELCH.

And I can cut the mutton to't.

SIR ANDREW AGUECHEEK.

And I think I have the back-trick simply as strong as any man in Illyria.

SIR TOBY BELCH.

Wherefore are these things hid? wherefore have these gifts a curtain before 'em? are they like to take dust, like Mistress Mall's picture? why dost thou not go to church in a galliard, and come home in a coranto?[4] My very walk should be a jig; I would not so much as make water but in a sink-a-pace. What dost thou mean? is it a world to hide virtues in? I did think, by the excellent constitution of thy leg, it was form'd under the star of a galliard.

---

[1] there's life in't: you have a chance.
[2] kickshawses: fantastical offerings.
[3] galliard: a lively dance.
[4] coranto: another quick, lively dance.

SIR ANDREW AGUECHEEK.

Ay, 'tis strong, and it does indifferent well in a flame-colour'd stock.[1] Shall we set about some revels?

SIR TOBY BELCH.

What shall we do else? were we not born under Taurus?

SIR ANDREW AGUECHEEK.

Taurus![2] that's sides and heart.

SIR TOBY BELCH.

No, sir; it is legs and thighs. Let me see thee caper [SIR ANDREW *dances*]: ha! higher: ha, ha! excellent!     [*Exeunt..*

## SCENE IV.

*The* DUKE'S *palace.*

*Enter* VALENTINE, *and* VIOLA *in man's attire.*

VALENTINE.

If the duke continue these favours towards you, Cesario, you are like to be much advanced: he hath known you but three days, and already you are no stranger.

VIOLA.

You either fear his humour or my negligence, that you call in question[3] the continuance of his love: is he inconstant, sir, in his favours?

VALENTINE.

No, believe me.

VIOLA.

I thank you. Here comes the count.

*Enter* DUKE, CURIO, *and* ATTENDANTS.

DUKE OF ILLYRIA.

Who saw Cesario, ho?

---

[1] stock: stocking.
[2] Taurus: the sign of the bull in the Zodiac.
[3] call/in question: to question or doubt.

VIOLA.

On your attendance, my lord; here.

DUKE OF ILLYRIA.

Stand you awhile aloof.[1]—Cesario,
Thou know'st no less but all; I have unclaspt[2]
To thee the book even of my secret soul:
Therefore, good youth, address thy gait unto her,[3]
Be not denied access, stand at her doors,
And tell them, there thy fixed foot shall grow
Till thou have audience.

VIOLA.

             Sure, my noble lord,
If she be so abandon'd to her sorrow
As it is spoke, she never will admit me.

DUKE OF ILLYRIA.

Be clamorous, and leap all civil bounds,
Rather than make unprofited return.

VIOLA.

Say I do speak with her, my lord, what then?

DUKE OF ILLYRIA.

O, then unfold the passion of my love,
Surprise her with discourse of my dear faith!
It shall become thee well to act my woes;
She will attend it better in thy youth
Than in a nuncio[4] of more grave aspect.

VIOLA.

I think not so, my lord.

DUKE OF ILLYRIA.

             Dear lad, believe it;
For they shall yet belie thy happy years,
That say thou art a man: Diana's[5] lip
Is not more smooth and rubious;[6] thy small pipe

---

[1] aloof: apart.
[2] unclaspt: opened.
[3] address thy gait unto her: go to her.
[4] nuncio: official messenger, or ambassador.
[5] Diana: virgin goddess of the hunt.
[6] rubious: red.

Is as the maiden's organ, shrill and sound;
And all is semblative[1] a woman's part.
I know thy constellation is right apt
For this affair:[2]—some four or five attend him;
All, if you will; for I myself am best
When least in company:—prosper well in this,
And thou shalt live as freely as thy lord,
To call his fortunes thine.

VIOLA.

                    I'll do my best
To woo your lady:—[*aside*] yet, a barful strife! [3]
Whoe'er I woo, myself would be his wife.          [*Exeunt.*

## SCENE V.

### OLIVIA'S *house.*

*Enter* MARIA *and* CLOWN.

MARIA.

Nay, either tell me where thou hast been, or I will not open
my lips so wide as a bristle may enter in way of thy excuse:
my lady will hang thee for thy absence.

CLOWN.

Let her hang me: he that is well hang'd in this world need
to fear no colours.[4]

MARIA.

Make that good.[5]

CLOWN.

He shall see none to fear.

MARIA.

A good lenten answer:[6] I can tell thee where that saying was
born, of,—I fear no colours.

CLOWN.

Where, good Mistress Mary?

---

[1] semblative: resembling. [2] thy constellation is right apt/ For this
affair: the stars favor your affair. [3] barful strife: an action with
many obstacles. [4] colours: flags. [5] Make that good: prove it. [6] lenten
answer: weak answer; lacking in substance: i.e., Lenten food.

MARIA.

In the wars; and that may you be bold to say in your foolery.

CLOWN.

Well, God give them wisdom that have it; and those that are fools, let them use their talents.[1]

MARIA.

Yet you will be hang'd for being so long absent; or, to be turn'd away,—is not that as good as a hanging to you?

CLOWN.

Many a good hanging prevents a bad marriage; and, for turning away, let summer bear it out.[2]

MARIA.

You are resolute, then?

CLOWN.

Not so, neither; but I am resolved on two points.

MARIA.

That if one break, the other will hold; or, if both break, your gaskins[3] fall.

CLOWN.

Apt, in good faith; very apt. Well, go thy way; if Sir Toby would leave drinking, thou wert as witty a piece of Eve's flesh[4] as any in Illyria.

MARIA.

Peace, you rogue, no more o'that. Here comes my lady: make your excuse wisely, you were best.                    [Exit.

CLOWN.

Wit, an't be thy will, put me into good fooling! Those wits, that think they have thee, do very oft prove fools; and I, that

---

[1] God give them wisdom that have it; and those that are/fools, let them use their talents: May the wise ones use their knowledge to the best advantage; fools must dissemble.

[2] bear it out: make bearable.

[3] gaskins: gaiters.

[4] Eve's flesh: woman.

am sure I lack thee, may pass for a wise man: for what says
Quinapalus?[1] 'Better a witty fool than a foolish wit.'

*Enter* LADY OLIVIA *with* MALVOLIO.

God bless thee, lady!

OLIVIA.

Take the fool away.

CLOWN.

Do you not hear, fellows? Take away the lady.

OLIVIA.

Go to, y'are a dry fool: I'll no more of you: besides, you grow
dishonest.

CLOWN.

Two faults, madonna, that drink and good counsel will
amend: for give the dry fool drink, then is the fool not dry:
bid the dishonest man mend himself; if he mend, he is no
longer dishonest: if he cannot, let the botcher[2] mend him:
any thing that's mended is but patcht: virtue that transgresses
is but patcht with sin; and sin that amends is but patcht with
virtue: if that this simple syllogism will serve, so;[3] if it will
not, what remedy? As there is no true cuckold but calamity,[4]
so beauty's a flower.—The lady bade take away the fool; therefore, I say again, take her away.

OLIVIA.

Sir, I bade them take away you.

CLOWN.

Misprision[5] in the highest degree!—Lady, *cucullus non facit
monachum*;[6] that's as much to say as, I wear not motley in
my brain. Good madonna, give me leave to prove you a fool.

---

[1] Quinapalus: a mythical sage invented for the occasion by the
clown Feste. [2] botcher: one who repairs or patches. [3] so: very well.
[4] As there is no true cuckold but calamity: since man is wedded to
Fortune, when Fortune fails, he is indeed a cuckold (a man whose
wife is unfaithful). [5] misprision: mistake; misunderstand. [6] cucullus
non facit/monachum: a cowl does not make a monk; i.e., his fool's
costume does not make the clown a fool.

OLIVIA.

Can you do it?

CLOWN.

Dexteriously, good madonna.

OLIVIA.

Make your proof.

CLOWN.

I must catechize you for it, madonna: good my mouse of virtue, answer me.

OLIVIA.

Well, sir, for want of other idleness,[1] I'll bide your proof.

CLOWN.

Good madonna, why mourn'st thou?

OLIVIA.

Good fool, for my brother's death.

CLOWN.

I think his soul is in hell, madonna.

OLIVIA.

I know his soul is in heaven, fool.

CLOWN.

The more fool, madonna, to mourn for your brother's soul being in heaven.—Take away the fool, gentlemen.

OLIVIA.

What think you of this fool, Malvolio? doth he not mend? [2]

MALVOLIO.

Yes, and shall do till the pangs of death shake him: infirmity, that decays the wise, doth ever make the better fool.[3]

CLOWN.

God send you, sir, a speedy infirmity, for the better increasing your folly! Sir Toby will be sworn that I am no fox; but he will not pass his word for twopence that you are no fool.

---

[1] for want of other idleness, I'll bide your proof: for lack of something better to do, I'll listen to your explanation.

[2] mend: get better; improve.

[3] infirmity,/ that decays the wise, doth ever make the better fool: age weakens the intellect of the wise and makes even bigger fools of dunces.

OLIVIA.

How say you to that, Malvolio?

MALVOLIO.

I marvel your ladyship takes delight in such a barren[1] rascal: I saw him put down[2] the other day with an ordinary fool, that has no more brain than a stone. Look you now, he's out of his guard[3] already; unless you laugh and minister occasion[4] to him, he is gagg'd. I protest, I take these wise men, that crow so at these set kind of fools, no better than the fools' zanies.

OLIVIA.

O, you are sick of self-love, Malvolio, and taste with a distemper'd appetite. To be generous, guiltless, and of free disposition, is to take those things for bird-bolts[5] that you deem cannon-bullets: there is no slander in an allow'd fool, though he do nothing but rail; nor no railing in a known discreet man, though he do nothing but reprove.

CLOWN.

Now Mercury endue thee with leasing,[6] for thou speak'st well of fools!

*Enter* MARIA.

MARIA.

Madam, there is at the gate a young gentleman much desires to speak with you.

OLIVIA.

From the Count Orsino, is it?

MARIA.

I know not, madam: 'tis a fair young man, and well attended.

---

[1] barren: mentally dull; stupid. [2] put down: bested. [3] out of his guard: a fencing term; helpless. [4] minister occasion: supply reason or opportunity. [5] bird-bolts: short, blunt arrows, to be shot from a crossbow at birds without piercing them. [6] Mercury endue thee with leasing: the god Mercury presided over everything requiring skill and dexterity (even trickery); hence, endow you with the ability to lie.

OLIVIA.

Who of my people hold him in delay?

MARIA.

Sir Toby, madam, your kinsman.

OLIVIA.

Fetch him off, I pray you; he speaks nothing but madman:
fie on him! [*Exit* MARIA.] Go you, Malvolio: if it be a suit
from the count, I am sick, or not at home; what you will, to
dismiss it. [*Exit* MALVOLIO.] Now you see, sir, how your fooling grows old,[1] and people dislike it.

CLOWN.

Thou hast spoke for us, madonna, as if thy eldest son should
be a fool; whose skull Jove[2] cram with brains! for—here he
comes—one of thy kin has a most weak *pia mater*.[3]

*Enter* SIR TOBY.

OLIVIA.

By mine honour, half drunk.—What is he at the gate, cousin?

SIR TOBY BELCH.

A gentleman.

OLIVIA.

A gentleman! what gentleman?

SIR TOBY BELCH.

'Tis a gentleman here—a plague o'these pickle-herring!—
How now, sot! [4]

CLOWN.

Good Sir Toby!—

OLIVIA.

Cousin, cousin, how have you come so early by this lethargy?

---

[1] old: antiquated.
[2] Jove: the god Jove or Jupiter.
[3] pia mater: the membrane covering the brain (the brain itself).
[4] sot: fool; simpleton.

SIR TOBY BELCH.

Lechery! I defy lechery. There's one at the gate.

OLIVIA.

Ay, marry, what is he?

SIR TOBY BELCH.

Let him be the devil, an he will, I care not: give me faith,[1]
say I. Well, it's all one.　　　　　　　　　　　[*Exit.*

OLIVIA.

What's a drunken man like, fool?

CLOWN.

Like a drown'd man, a fool, and a madman: one draught
above heat[2] makes him a fool; the second mads him; and a
third drowns him.

OLIVIA.

Go thou and seek the crowner,[3] and let him sit o' my coz;[4]
for he's in the third degree of drink,—he's drown'd: go, look
after him.

CLOWN.

He is but mad yet, madonna; and the fool shall look to the
madman.　　　　　　　　　　　　　　　　　　[*Exit.*

*Enter* MALVOLIO.

MALVOLIO.

Madam, yond young fellow swears he will speak with you. I
told him you were sick; he takes on him[5] to understand so
much, and therefore comes to speak with you: I told him you
were asleep; he seems to have a foreknowledge of that too,
and therefore comes to speak with you. What is to be said
to him, lady? he's fortified against any denial.

OLIVIA.

Tell him he shall not speak with me.

---

[1] give me faith: give me strength.
[2] one draught/above heat: one more drink than his capacity.
[3] crowner: coroner.
[4] sit o' my coz: hold an inquest for my cousin.
[5] he takes on him: he pretends.

MALVOLIO.

Has been told so; and he says, he'll stand at your door like
a sheriff's post,[1] and be the supporter to a bench, but he'll
speak with you.

OLIVIA.

What kind o'man is he?

MALVOLIO.

Why, of mankind.

OLIVIA.

What manner of man?

MALVOLIO.

Of very ill manner; he'll speak with you, will you or no.

OLIVIA.

Of what personage and years is he?

MALVOLIO.

Not yet old enough for a man, nor young enough for a boy;
as a squash is before 'tis a peascod,[2] or a codling[3] when 'tis
almost an apple: 'tis with him e'en standing water,[4] between
boy and man. He is very well-favour'd, and he speaks very
shrewishly; one would think his mother's milk were scarce out
of him.

OLIVIA.

Let him approach: call in my gentlewoman.

MALVOLIO.

Gentlewoman, my lady calls.        [*Exit.*

*Enter* MARIA.

OLIVIA.

Give me my veil: come, throw it o'er my face. We'll once
more hear Orsino's embassy.

*Enter* VIOLA.

VIOLA.

The honourable lady of the house, which is she?

---

[1] sheriff's post: guard post.

[2] peascod: pea pod.

[3] codling: immature apple; i.e., callow youth.

[4] standing water: between ebb and flow; at the halfway point between boy and man.

OLIVIA.

Speak to me; I shall answer for her. Your will?

VIOLA.

Most radiant, exquisite, and unmatchable beauty,—I pray
you, tell me if this be the lady of the house, for I never saw
her: I would be loth to cast away my speech; for, besides that
it is excellently well penn'd, I have taken great pains to con[1]
it. Good beauties, let me sustain no scorn; I am very comp-
tible,[2] even to the least sinister usage.

OLIVIA.

Whence came you, sir?

VIOLA.

I can say little more than I have studied, and that question's
out of my part. Good gentle one, give me modest[3] assurance
if you be the lady of the house, that I may proceed in my
speech.

OLIVIA.

Are you a comedian? [4]

VIOLA.

No, my profound heart: and yet, by the very fangs of malice
I swear I am not that I play. Are you the lady of the house?

OLIVIA.

If I do not usurp myself, I am.

VIOLA.

Most certain, if you are she, you do usurp yourself; for, what
is yours to bestow is not yours to reserve. But this is from my
commission:[5] I will on with my speech in your praise, and
then show you the heart of my message.

OLIVIA.

Come to what is important in't: I forgive you the praise.

---

[1] con: peruse: commit to memory.
[2] comp/tible: sensitive.
[3] modest: moderate.
[4] comedian: performer; actor.
[5] But this is from my commission: this is not part of my mission or
project.

VIOLA.

Alas, I took great pains to study it, and 'tis poetical.

OLIVIA.

It is the more like to be feign'd:[1] I pray you, keep it in. I
heard you were saucy at my gates; and allow'd your approach
rather to wonder at you than to hear you. If you be mad, be
gone; if you have reason, be brief: 'tis not that time of moon
with me to make one in so skipping[2] a dialogue.

MALVOLIO.

Will you hoist sail, sir? here lies your way.

VIOLA.

No, good swabber;[3] I am to hull[4] here a little longer. Some
mollification for your giant, sweet lady. Tell me your mind:
I am a messenger.

OLIVIA.

Sure, you have some hideous matter to deliver, when the
courtesy of it is so fearful. Speak your office.

VIOLA.

It alone concerns your ear. I bring no overture of war, no
taxation[5] of homage: I hold the olive in my hand; my words
are as full of peace as matter.

OLIVIA.

Yet you began rudely. What are you? what would you?

VIOLA.

The rudeness that hath appear'd in me have I learn'd from
my entertainment.[6] What I am, and what I would, are as
secret as maidenhead: to your ears, divinity;[7] to any other's,
profanation.

---

[1] feign'd: not genuine. [2] skipping: frivolous; light. [3] swabber: one
who scrubs decks. [4] hull: to idle: loaf about. [5] taxation: imposition.
[6] entertainment: reception. [7] divinity: godly conversation.

OLIVIA.

Give us the place alone: we will hear this divinity.    [*Exit*
MARIA.] Now, sir, what is your text?

VIOLA.

Most sweet lady,—

OLIVIA.

A comfortable doctrine, and much may be said of it. Where
lies your text?

VIOLA.

In Orsino's bosom.

OLIVIA.

In his bosom! In what chapter of his bosom?

VIOLA.

To answer by the method,[1] in the first of his heart.

OLIVIA.

O, I have read it: it is heresy. Have you no more to say?

VIOLA.

Good madam, let me see your face.

OLIVIA.

Have you any commission from your lord to negotiate with
my face? You are now out of your text:[2] but we will draw
the curtain, and show you the picture.[3] Look you, sir, such a
one I was, this presents: is't not well done?      [*Unveiling.*

VIOLA.

Excellently done, if God did all.

OLIVIA.

'Tis in grain,[4] sir; 'twill endure wind and weather.

VIOLA.

'Tis beauty truly blent, whose red and white
Nature's own sweet and cunning hand laid on:

---

[1] by the method: in the style of a preacher.
[2] out of your text: straying from the prescribed text; i.e., switching
from "heart" to "face."
[3] the picture: my face.
[4] grain: lasting color: crimson dye made from kermes (dried scales
found on the kermes oak).

Lady, you are the cruell'st she alive,
If you will lead these graces to the grave,
And leave the world no copy.

OLIVIA.

O, sir, I will not be so hard-hearted; I will give out divers
schedules of my beauty: it shall be inventoried, and every
particle and utensil labell'd [1] to my will:—as, item, two lips,
indifferent red; item, two gray eyes, with lids to them; item,
one neck, one chin, and so forth. Were you sent hither to
'praise[2] me?

VIOLA.

I see you what you are,—you are too proud;
But, if you were the devil, you are fair.
My lord and master loves you: O, such love
Could be but recompensed, though you were crown'd
The nonpareil of beauty!

OLIVIA.

How does he love me?

VIOLA.

With adorations, with fertile[3] tears,
With groans that thunder love, with sighs of fire.

OLIVIA.

Your lord does know my mind; I cannot love him:
Yet I suppose him virtuous, know him noble,
Of great estate, of fresh and stainless youth;
In voices well divulged,[4] free,[5] learn'd, and valiant;
And, in dimension and the shape of nature,[6]
A gracious person: but yet I cannot love him;
He might have took his answer long ago.

---

[1] labell'd: attached.
[2] 'praise: appraise.
[3] fertile: copious.
[4] In voices well divulged: well-known sources.
[5] free: openhanded; liberal.
[6] dimension and the shape of nature: physique.

VIOLA.

If I did love you in my master's flame,[1]
With such a suffering, such a deadly life,
In your denial I would find no sense;
I would not understand it.

OLIVIA.

                    Why, what would you?

VIOLA.

Make me a willow cabin at your gate,
And call upon my soul within the house;[2]
Write loyal cantons[3] of contemned [4] love,
And sing them loud even in the dead of night;
Holla your name to the reverberate hills,
And make the babbling gossip of the air
Cry out, 'Olivia!' O, you should not rest
Between the elements of air and earth,
But you should pity me!

OLIVIA.

You might do much. What is your parentage?

VIOLA.

Above my fortunes, yet my state is well:
I am a gentleman.

OLIVIA.

                 Get you to your lord;
I cannot love him: let him send no more;
Unless, perchance, you come to me again,
To tell me how he takes it. Fare you well:
I thank you for your pains: spend this for me.

VIOLA.

I am no fee'd post,[5] lady; keep your purse:
My master, not myself, lacks recompense.
Love make his heart of flint, that you shall love;
And let your fervour, like my master's, be

---

[1] flame: ardor.
[2] my soul within the house: meaning Olivia.
[3] cantons: from the musical term "cantos."
[4] contemned: despised.
[5] fee'd post: paid messenger.

Placed in contempt! Farewell, fair cruelty.    [*Exit.*

OLIVIA.
'What is your parentage?'
'Above my fortunes, yet my state is well:
I am a gentleman.' I'll be sworn thou art;
Thy tongue, thy face, thy limbs, actions, and spirit,
Do give thee fivefold blazon:[1]—not too fast;—
Soft, soft![2]—
Unless the master were the man.—How now!
Even so quickly may one catch the plague?
Methinks I feel this youth's perfections
With an invisible and subtle stealth
To creep in at mine eyes. Well, let it be.—
What, ho, Malvolio!

*Enter* MALVOLIO.

MALVOLIO.
                    Here, madam, at your service.
OLIVIA.
Run after that same peevish messenger,
The county's man:[3] he left this ring behind him,
Would I or not: tell him I'll none of it.
Desire him not to flatter with his lord,
Nor hold him up with hopes; I am not for him:
If that the youth will come this way to-morrow,
I'll give him reasons for't. Hie thee,[4] Malvolio.
MALVOLIO.
Madam, I will.    [*Exit.*
OLIVIA.
I do I know not what; and fear to find
Mine eye too great a flatterer for my mind.[5]
Fate, show thy force: ourselves we do not owe;
What is decreed must be,—and be this so!    [*Exit.*

---

[1] blazon: proclaim far and wide.
[2] soft: go easy.
[3] county's man: count's man.
[4] Hie thee: hurry.
[5] Mine eye too great a flatterer for my mind: my eyes say one thing, my mind another.

# Twelfth Night

## ACT 2

# ACT II

As the act opens, we meet Sebastian, Viola's twin brother whom she supposed to have been drowned but who has arrived safely in Illyria with Antonio, the captain of the wrecked ship. Sebastian decides to go to the Duke's court, but not Antonio, since he has enemies there. He will nevertheless keep watch over Sebastian's welfare. In the meantime, Olivia has sent Malvolio after Viola with a ring, which at once confirms what Viola suspects, that Olivia, thinking her a man, is in love with her. Malvolio upon his return so annoys the revelling Sir Toby, Sir Andrew, and the Clown that they decide, with Maria's help, to trick him into believing that Olivia loves him. They write a letter, purporting to come from Olivia, containing expressions of love and begging him to go "in yellow stockings and cross-gartered," both of which Olivia detests. They place the letter where he will find it, and watch in glee as he picks it up, reads, and is completely taken in. Meanwhile, at the Duke's palace, Viola's passion for Orsino grows under the stimulus of Feste's songs and music, so that she almost confesses her love for the Duke. But he, though he senses a strange bond between them, sends her off to Olivia on further errands of love.

# ACT II. Scene I.

## *The sea-coast.*

*Enter* ANTONIO *and* SEBASTIAN.

ANTONIO.

Will you stay no longer? nor will you not that I go with you?

SEBASTIAN.

By your patience,[1] no. My stars shine darkly over me: the malignancy of my fate might perhaps distemper[2] yours; therefore I shall crave of you your leave that I may bear my evils alone: it were a bad recompense for your love, to lay any of them on you.

ANTONIO.

Let me yet know of you whither you are bound.

SEBASTIAN.

No, sooth,[3] sir: my determinate voyage is mere extravagancy. But I perceive in you so excellent a touch of modesty, that you will not extort from me what I am willing to keep in; therefore it charges me in manners[4] the rather to express myself. You must know of me, then, Antonio, my name is Sebastian, which I call'd Roderigo. My father was that Sebastian of Messaline, whom I know you have heard of. He left behind him myself and a sister, both born in an hour:[5] if the heavens had been pleased, would we had so ended! but you, sir, alter'd that; for some hour before you took me from the breach[6] of the sea was my sister drown'd.

---

[1] By your patience: by your indulgence.
[2] distemper: disturb.
[3] sooth: in truth.
[4] charges me in manners: courtesy compels me.
[5] both born in an hour: twins born within the same hour.
[6] breach: surf.

ANTONIO.

Alas the day!

SEBASTIAN.

A lady, sir, though it was said she much resembled me, was
yet of many accounted beautiful: but, though I could not,
with such estimable wonder, overfar believe that, yet thus
far I will boldly publish[1] her,—she bore a mind that envy
could not but call fair. She is drown'd already, sir, with salt
water, though I seem to drown her remembrance again with
more.

ANTONIO.

Pardon me, sir, your bad entertainment.[2]

SEBASTIAN.

O good Antonio, forgive me your trouble!

ANTONIO.

If you will not murder me[3] for my love, let me be your
servant.

SEBASTIAN.

If you will not undo what you have done, that is, kill him
whom you have recover'd, desire it not. Fare ye well at once:
my bosom is full of kindness; and I am yet so near the manners of my mother,[4] that, upon the least occasion more, mine
eyes will tell tales of me. I am bound to the Count Orsino's
court: farewell.                                    [*Exit.*

ANTONIO.

The gentleness of all the gods go with thee!
I have many enemies in Orsino's court,
Else would I very shortly see thee there:
But, come what may, I do adore thee so,
That danger shall seem sport, and I will go.        [*Exit.*

---

[1] publish: expose.
[2] bad entertainment: poor reception.
[3] murder me: cut me off.
[4] manners of my mother: soft and womanly.

## Scene II.

### A *street*.

#### *Enter* VIOLA, MALVOLIO *following*.

MALVOLIO.

Were not you even now with the Countess Olivia?

VIOLA.

Even[1] now, sir; on a moderate pace I have since arrived but hither.

MALVOLIO.

She returns this ring to you, sir: you might have saved me my pains, to have taken it away yourself. She adds, moreover, that you should put your lord into a desperate[2] assurance she will none of him: and one thing more, that you be never so hardy to come again in his affairs, unless it be to report your lord's taking of this. Receive it so.

VIOLA.

She took no ring of me;—I'll none of it.

MALVOLIO.

Come, sir, you peevishly threw it to her; and her will is, it should be so return'd: if it be worth stooping for, there it lies in your eye; if not, be it his that finds it.     [*Exit.*

VIOLA.

I left no ring with her: what means this lady?
Fortune forbid, my outside have not charm'd her!
She made good view of me; indeed, so much,
That, sure, methought, her eyes had lost her tongue,[3]
For she did speak in starts distractedly.
She loves me, sure; the cunning of her passion

---

[1] Even: just.

[2] desperate: without hope.

[3] her eyes had lost her tongue: the sight of him left her speechless.

Invites me in this churlish messenger.
None of my lord's ring! why, he sent her none.
I am the man: if it be so, as 'tis,
Poor lady, she were better love a dream.
Disguise, I see, thou art a wickedness,
Wherein the pregnant enemy[1] does much.
How easy is it for the proper-false[2]
In women's waxen hearts to set their forms!
Alas, our frailty is the cause, not we!
For such as we are made of, such we be.
How will this fadge? [3] my master loves her dearly;
And I, poor monster, fond as much on him;
And she, mistaken, seems to dote on me.
What will become of this? As I am man,
My state is desperate for my master's love;
As I am woman,—now, alas the day!—
What thriftless[4] sighs shall poor Olivia breathe!
O Time, thou must untangle this, not I;
It is too hard a knot for me t'untie!            [*Exit.*

## SCENE III.

### OLIVIA's *house.*

*Enter* SIR TOBY *and* SIR ANDREW.

SIR TOBY BELCH.

Approach, Sir Andrew: not to be a-bed after midnight is to
be up betimes;[5] and *diluculo surgere*,[6] thou know'st,—

SIR ANDREW AGUECHEEK.

Nay, by my troth, I know not: but I know, to be up late is to
be up late.

---

[1] **pregnant enemy:** ready enemy (the Devil). [2] **the proper-false:** a
man outwardly good but inherently false. [3] **fadge:** suit; agree (be
compatible). [4] **thriftless:** lacking usefulness or worth. [5] **betimes:**
early. [6] **diluculo surgere:** the beginning of a Latin phrase—"Diluculo surgere saluberrimum est"—"To rise early is most healthful."

SIR TOBY BELCH.

A false conclusion: I hate it as an unfill'd can. To be up after midnight, and to go to bed then, is early: so that to go to bed after midnight is to go to bed betimes. Does not our life[1] consist of the four elements? [2]

SIR ANDREW AGUECHEEK.

Faith, so they say; but, I think, it rather consists of eating and drinking.

SIR TOBY BELCH.

Th'art a scholar: let us therefore eat and drink.—Marian, I say! a stoup[3] of wine!

SIR ANDREW AGUECHEEK.

Here comes the fool, i'faith.

*Enter* CLOWN.

CLOWN.

How now, my hearts! did you never see the picture of We Three?

SIR TOBY BELCH.

Welcome, ass. Now let's have a catch.[4]

SIR ANDREW AGUECHEEK.

By my troth, the fool has an excellent breast.[5] I had rather than forty shillings I had such a leg, and so sweet a breath to sing, as the fool has. In sooth, thou wast in very gracious fooling last night, when thou spokest of Pigrogromitus, of the Vapians passing the equinoctial of Queubus:[6] 'twas very good, i'faith. I sent thee sixpence for thy leman:[7] hadst it?

CLOWN.

I did impeticos thy gratillity;[8] for Malvolio's nose is no whip-stock; my lady has a white hand, and the Myrmidons[9] are no bottle-ale houses.

---

[1] **our life:** make-up of the human body. [2] **four elements:** air, earth, fire, and water. [3] **stoup:** flagon; a drinking vessel. [4] **catch:** song (literally, a ludicrous or coarse round). [5] **breast:** voice. [6] **Pigrogromi-tus, of/the Vapians passing the equinoctial of Queubus:** double talk. [7] **leman:** sweetheart or mistress. [8] **impeticos thy gratillity:** more double talk. [9] **Myrmidons:** legendary Thessalian troops accompanying Achilles to the Trojan war.

SIR ANDREW AGUECHEEK.

Excellent! why, this is the best fooling, when all is done.
Now, a song.

SIR TOBY BELCH.

Come on; there is sixpence for you: let's have a song.

SIR ANDREW AGUECHEEK.

There's a testril [1] of me too; if one knight give a—

CLOWN.

Would you have a love-song, or a song of good life? [2]

SIR TOBY BELCH.

A love-song, a love-song.

SIR ANDREW AGUECHEEK.

Ay, ay: I care not for good life.

CLOWN [sings].

    O mistress mine, where are you roaming?
    O, stay and hear; your true-love's coming,
       That can sing both high and low:
    Trip no further, pretty sweeting;
    Journeys end in lovers' meeting,
       Every wise man's son doth know.

SIR ANDREW AGUECHEEK.

Excellent good, i' faith.

SIR TOBY BELCH.

Good, good.

CLOWN.

    What is love? 'tis not hereafter;
    Present mirth hath present laughter;
       What's to come is still unsure:
    In delay there lies no plenty;
    Then come kiss me, sweet-and-twenty,
       Youth's a stuff will not endure.

---

[1] testril: sixpence.
[2] song of good life: "good" here means moral.

SIR ANDREW AGUECHEEK.

A mellifluous voice, as I am true knight.

SIR TOBY BELCH.

A contagious breath.[1]

SIR ANDREW AGUECHEEK.

Very sweet and contagious, i'faith.

SIR TOBY BELCH.

To hear by the nose, it is dulcet in contagion. But shall we make the welkin[2] dance indeed? shall we rouse the night-owl in a catch that will draw three souls out of one weaver? [3] shall we do that?

SIR ANDREW AGUECHEEK.

An you love me, let's do't: I am dog[4] at a catch.

CLOWN.

By'r lady, sir, and some dogs will catch well.

SIR ANDREW AGUECHEEK.

Most certain. Let our catch be, 'Thou knave.'

CLOWN.

'Hold thy peace, thou knave,' knight? I shall be constrain'd in't to call thee knave, knight.

SIR ANDREW AGUECHEEK.

'Tis not the first time I have constrain'd one to call me knave. Begin, fool: it begins, 'Hold thy peace.'

CLOWN.

I shall never begin, if I hold my peace.

SIR ANDREW AGUECHEEK.

Good, i'faith. Come, begin.          [Catch sung.

### Enter MARIA.

MARIA.

What a caterwauling do you keep here! If my lady have not call'd up her steward Malvolio, and bid him turn you out of doors, never trust me.

---

[1] contagious breath: catching voice (a pun on "catch").

[2] welkin: the heavens.

[3] draw three souls out of one weaver: attempt to do the impossible.

[4] dog: slyly clever.

**SIR TOBY BELCH.**

My lady's a Cataian,[1] we are politicians,[2] Malvolio's a Peg-a-Ramsey,[3] and 'Three merry men be we.' Am not I consanguineous?[4] am I not of her blood? Tilly-vally,[5] lady!
[*Sings*] 'There dwelt a man in Babylon, lady, lady!'

**CLOWN.**

Beshrew[6] me, the knight's in admirable fooling.

**SIR ANDREW AGUECHEEK.**

Ay, he does well enough if he be disposed, and so do I too: he does it with a better grace, but I do it more natural.

**SIR TOBY BELCH.**

'O, the twelfth day of December,—'

**MARIA.**

For the love o' God, peace!

*Enter* MALVOLIO.

**MALVOLIO.**

My masters, are you mad? or what are you? Have you no wit, manners, nor honesty, but to gabble like tinkers at this time of night? Do ye make an ale-house of my lady's house, that ye squeak out your cosiers'[7] catches without any mitigation or remorse of voice? Is there no respect of place, persons, nor time, in you?

**SIR TOBY BELCH.**

We did keep time, sir, in our catches. Sneck-up![8]

**MALVOLIO.**

Sir Toby, I must be round[9] with you. My lady bade me tell you, that, though she harbours you as her kinsman, she's nothing allied to your disorders.[10] If you can separate yourself and your misdemeanours, you are welcome to the house; if

---

[1] **Cataian:** a native of China (Cathay); used in a derogatory way; a sharper. [2] **politicians:** schemers, in this sense. [3] **Peg-a-Ramsey:** the name of a song. [4] **consanguineous:** of the same blood. [5] **Tilly-vally:** meaningless nonsense. [6] **Beshrew:** mild oath (evil befall!). [7] **cosiers:** tailors. [8] **Sneck-up:** interjection, go hang! [9] **round:** blunt. [10] **she's/nothing allied to your dis-orders:** she does not approve of your actions.

not, an it would please you to take leave of her, she is very willing to bid you farewell.

SIR TOBY BELCH.

'Farewell, dear heart, since I must needs be gone.'

MARIA.

Nay, good Sir Toby.

CLOWN.

'His eyes do show his days are almost done.'

MALVOLIO.

Is't even so?

SIR TOBY BELCH.

'But I will never die.'

CLOWN.

Sir Toby, there you lie.

MALVOLIO.

This is much credit to you.

SIR TOBY BELCH.

'Shall I bid him go?'

CLOWN.

'What an if you do?'

SIR TOBY BELCH.

'Shall I bid him go, and spare not?'

CLOWN.

'O, no, no, no, no, you dare not.'

SIR TOBY BELCH.

Out o'time, sir? ye lie.—Art any more than a steward? Dost thou think, because thou art virtuous, there shall be no more cakes and ale?

CLOWN.

Yes, by Saint Anne; and ginger shall be hot i'th' mouth too.

SIR TOBY BELCH.

Th'art i'th'right.—Go, sir, rub your chain[1] with crumbs.— A stoup of wine, Maria!

---

[1] chain: steward's chain.

MALVOLIO.

Mistress Mary, if you prized my lady's favour at any thing more than contempt, you would not give means for this uncivil rule:[1] she shall know of it, by this hand.          [Exit.

MARIA.

Go shake your ears.[2]

SIR ANDREW AGUECHEEK.

'Twere as good a deed as to drink when a man's a-hungry,[3] to challenge him the field, and then to break promise with him, and make a fool of him.

SIR TOBY BELCH.

Do't, knight: I'll write thee a challenge; or I'll deliver thy indignation to him by word of mouth.

MARIA.

Sweet Sir Toby, be patient for to-night; since the youth of the count's was to-day with my lady, she is much out of quiet.[4] For Monsieur Malvolio, let me alone with him: if I do not gull [5] him into a nayword, and make him a common recreation, do not think I have wit enough to lie straight in my bed: I know I can do it.

SIR TOBY BELCH.

Possess us,[6] possess us; tell us something of him.

MARIA.

Marry, sir, sometimes he is a kind of puritan.

SIR ANDREW AGUECHEEK.

O, if I thought that, I'ld beat him like a dog!

SIR TOBY BELCH.

What, for being a puritan? thy exquisite reason, dear knight?

---

[1] uncivil rule: bad behavior.
[2] shake your ears: shake your ears like an ass or a donkey.
[3] drink when a man's a-hungry: get him drunk.
[4] out of quiet: disturbed.
[5] gull: trick.
[6] possess us: inform us.

SIR ANDREW AGUECHEEK.

I have no exquisite reason for't, but I have reason good enough.

MARIA.

The devil a puritan that he is, or any thing constantly,[1] but a time-pleaser; an affection'd ass, that cons state without book,[2] and utters it by great swarths:[3] the best persuaded of himself,[4] so cramm'd, as he thinks, with excellencies, that it is his grounds of faith that all that look on him love him; and on that vice in him will my revenge find notable cause to work.

SIR TOBY BELCH.

What wilt thou do?

MARIA.

I will drop in his way some obscure epistles of love; wherein, by the colour of his beard, the shape of his leg, the manner of his gait, the expressure[5] of his eye, forehead, and complexion, he shall find himself most feelingly personated:[6] I can write very like my lady, your niece; on a forgotten matter we can hardly make distinction of our hands.

SIR TOBY BELCH.

Excellent! I smell a device.

SIR ANDREW AGUECHEEK.

I have't in my nose too.

SIR TOBY BELCH.

He shall think, by the letters that thou wilt drop, that they come from my niece, and that she's in love with him.

MARIA.

My purpose is, indeed, a horse of that colour.

---

[1] constantly: unfailingly. [2] cons state without/book: knows manners without reading about them. [3] swarths: swaths; puts on a big display. [4] best persuaded of/himself: has a very high opinion of himself. [5] expressure: expression. [6] feelingly personated: convincingly portrayed.

SIR TOBY BELCH.

And your horse now would make him an ass.

MARIA.

Ass, I doubt not.

SIR ANDREW AGUECHEEK.

O, 'twill be admirable!

MARIA.

Sport royal, I warrant you: I know my physic will work with him. I will plant you two, and let the fool make a third, where he shall find the letter: observe his construction of it. For this night, to bed, and dream on the event.[1] Farewell.

SIR TOBY BELCH.

Good night, Penthesilea.[2]                    [*Exit* MARIA.

SIR ANDREW AGUECHEEK.

Before me,[3] she's a good wench.

SIR TOBY BELCH.

She's a beagle,[4] true-bred, and one that adores me: what o'that?

SIR ANDREW AGUECHEEK.

I was adored once too.

SIR TOBY BELCH.

Let's to bed, knight.—Thou hadst need send for more money.

SIR ANDREW AGUECHEEK.

If I cannot recover your niece, I am a foul way out.[5]

SIR TOBY BELCH.

Send for money, knight: if thou hast her not i'th'end, call me cut.[6]

SIR ANDREW AGUECHEEK.

If I do not, never trust me, take it how you will.

---

[1] on the event: of the outcome.
[2] Penthesilea: queen of the Amazons, brave and able in battle.
[3] Before me: I attest.
[4] beagle: a term of opprobrium.
[5] foul way out: broke; out of money.
[6] cut: gelded.

SIR TOBY BELCH.
Come, come; I'll go burn some sack;[1] 'tis too late to go to
bed now: come, knight; come, knight.            [*Exeunt.*

## SCENE IV.

*The DUKE's palace.*

*Enter DUKE, VIOLA, CURIO, and others.*

DUKE OF ILLYRIA.
Give me some music:—now, good morrow, friends:—
Now, good Cesario, but that piece of song,
That old and antique song we heard last night:
Methought it did relieve my passion much,
More than light airs and recollected terms
Of these most brisk and giddy-paced times:—
Come, but one verse.
CURIO.
He is not here, so please your lordship, that should sing it.
DUKE OF ILLYRIA.
Who was it?
CURIO.
Feste, the jester, my lord; a fool that the Lady Olivia's father
took much delight in: he is about the house.
DUKE OF ILLYRIA.
Seek him out: and play the tune the while.
                              [*Exit CURIO. Music plays.*
Come hither, boy: if ever thou shalt love,
In the sweet pangs of it remember me;
For such as I am all true lovers are,
Unstaid [2] and skittish in all motions else,
Save in the constant image of the creature
That is beloved.—How dost thou like this tune?

---

[1] burn some sack: heat some wine.
[2] unstaid: unstable.

VIOLA.

It gives a very echo to the seat[1]
Where Love is throned.

DUKE OF ILLYRIA.

       Thou dost speak masterly: 
My life upon't, young though thou art, thine eye
Hath stay'd upon some favour[2] that it loves;—
Hath it not, boy?

VIOLA.

     A little, by your favour.

DUKE OF ILLYRIA.

What kind of woman is't?

VIOLA.

       Of your complexion.[3]

DUKE OF ILLYRIA.

She is not worth thee, then. What years, i'faith?

VIOLA.

About your years, my lord.

DUKE OF ILLYRIA.

Too old, by heaven: let still the woman take
An elder than herself; so wears[4] she to him,
So sways she level [5] in her husband's heart:
For, boy, however we do praise ourselves,
Our fancies[6] are more giddy and unfirm,
More longing, wavering, sooner lost and worn,
Than women's are.

VIOLA.

     I think it well, my lord.

DUKE OF ILLYRIA.

Then let thy love be younger than thyself,
Or thy affection cannot hold the bent;[7]

---

[1] echo to the seat: touches the heart. [2] stay'd upon some favour: gazed on some face. [3] complexion: nature; disposition. [4] wears: molds herself in his pattern. [5] sways she level: remains constant. [6] fancies: ideas of love. [7] hold the bent: remain at its high pitch.

For women are as roses, whose fair flower
Being once display'd, doth fall that very hour.

    VIOLA.

And so they are: alas, that they are so,—
To die, even when they to perfection grow!

       *Enter* CURIO *and* CLOWN.

    DUKE OF ILLYRIA.

O, fellow, come, the song we had last night.—
Mark it, Cesario; it is old and plain:
The spinsters and the knitters in the sun,
And the free[1] maids that weave their thread with bones,
Do use to chant it: it is silly sooth,
And dallies[2] with the innocence of love,
Like the old age.[3]

    CLOWN.

Are you ready, sir?

    DUKE OF ILLYRIA.

Ay; prithee, sing.                     [*Music.*

    CLOWN.

  Come away, come away, death,
    And in sad cypress[4] let me be laid;
  Fly away, fly away, breath;
    I am slain by a fair cruel maid.
  My shroud of white, stuck all with yew,
      O, prepare it!
  My part of death, no one so true

      Did share it.
  Not a flower, not a flower sweet,
    On my black coffin let there be strown;
  Not a friend, not a friend greet[5]

---

[1] free: carefree.
[2] dallies: plays.
[3] Like the old age: as of old.
[4] sad cypress: cypress coffin.
[5] greet: lament.

My poor corpse, where my bones shall be thrown:
A thousand thousand sighs to save,
Lay me, O, where
Sad true lover never find my grave,
To weep there!

DUKE OF ILLYRIA.

There's for thy pains.

CLOWN.

No pains, sir; I take pleasure in singing, sir.

DUKE OF ILLYRIA.

I'll pay thy pleasure, then.

CLOWN.

Truly, sir, and pleasure will be paid, one time or another.

DUKE OF ILLYRIA.

Give me now leave to leave thee.

CLOWN.

Now, the melancholy god protect thee; and the tailor make thy doublet[1] of changeable taffeta, for thy mind is a very opal![2] I would have men of such constancy put to sea, that their business might be every thing, and their intent[3] every where; for that's it that always makes a good voyage of nothing. Farewell. [*Exit.*

DUKE OF ILLYRIA.

Let all the rest give place.[4] [*Exeunt* CURIO *and* ATTENDANTS.
Once more, Cesario,
Get thee to yond same sovereign cruelty:[5]
Tell her, my love, more noble than the world,
Prizes not quantity of dirty lands;
The parts that Fortune hath bestow'd upon her,
Tell her, I hold as giddily as Fortune;[6]

---

[1] doublet: close-fitting jacket. [2] is a very opal: is very changeable.
[3] intent: goal. [4] give place: leave. [5] same sovereign cruelty: the woman who so cruelly rules over his heart. [6] giddily as Fortune: as inconstant as Fortune; reference to fickle Fortune.

But 'tis that miracle and queen of gems,
That nature pranks her in,[1] attracts my soul.

VIOLA.

But if she cannot love you, sir?

DUKE OF ILLYRIA.

I cannot be so answer'd.

VIOLA.

　　　　　　　　Sooth,[2] but you must.
Say that some lady—as, perhaps, there is—
Hath for your love as great a pang of heart
As you have for Olivia: you cannot love her;
You tell her so; must she not, then, be answer'd?

DUKE OF ILLYRIA.

There is no woman's sides
Can bide[3] the beating of so strong a passion
As love doth give my heart; no woman's heart
So big, to hold so much; they lack retention.
Alas, their love may be call'd appetite,—
No motion of the liver,[4] but the palate,—
That suffer surfeit, cloyment,[5] and revolt;[6]
But mine is all as hungry as the sea,
And can digest as much: make no compare
Between that love a woman can bear me
And that I owe Olivia.

VIOLA.

　　　　　　　Ay, but I know,—

DUKE OF ILLYRIA.

What dost thou know?

VIOLA.

Too well what love women to men may owe:
In faith, they are as true of heart as we.
My father had a daughter loved a man,
As it might be, perhaps, were I a woman,

---

[1] queen of gems,/ That nature pranks her in: the rare beauty with which Nature has endowed her. [2] sooth: in truth. [3] bide: endure; abide. [4] liver: the liver was thought to be the seat of the emotions. [5] cloyment: satiation; cloying. [6] revolt: disgust.

I should your lordship.

DUKE OF ILLYRIA.

              And what's her history?

VIOLA.

A blank, my lord. She never told her love,
But let concealment, like a worm i'th'bud,
Feed on her damask[1] cheek: she pined in thought;
And, with a green and yellow melancholy,[2]
She sat like Patience on a monument,
Smiling at grief. Was not this love indeed?
We men may say more, swear more: but, indeed,
Our shows are more than will;[3] for still we prove
Much in our vows, but little in our love.

DUKE OF ILLYRIA.

But died thy sister of her love, my boy?

VIOLA.

I am all the daughters of my father's house,
And all the brothers too;—and yet I know not.—
Sir, shall I to this lady?

DUKE OF ILLYRIA.

              Ay, that's the theme.
To her in haste; give her this jewel; say,
My love can give no place, bide no denay.[4]          [Exeunt.


## SCENE V.

### OLIVIA's garden.

#### Enter SIR TOBY, SIR ANDREW, and FABIAN.

SIR TOBY BELCH.

Come thy ways, Signior Fabian.

FABIAN.

Nay, I'll come: if I lose a scruple[5] of this sport, let me be
boil'd to death with melancholy.

---

[1] damask: her cheek is likened to the damask rose cultivated in
Asia Minor as a source of attar of roses. [2] melancholy: gloomy
mental state. [3] Our shows are more than will: we pretend a love
greater than our real ardor. [4] denay: denial. [5] scruple: small part.

SIR TOBY BELCH.

Wouldst thou not be glad to have the niggardly rascally sheep-biter[1] come by some notable shame?

FABIAN.

I would exult, man: you know he brought me out o'favour with my lady about a bear-baiting here.

SIR TOBY BELCH.

To anger him, we'll have the bear again; and we will fool him black and blue:—shall we not, Sir Andrew?

SIR ANDREW AGUECHEEK.

An we do not, it is pity of our lives.

SIR TOBY BELCH.

Here comes the little villain.

*Enter* MARIA.

How now, my metal of India! [2]

MARIA.

Get ye all three into the box-tree: Malvolio's coming down this walk: he has been yonder i'the sun practising behaviour to his own shadow this half-hour: observe him, for the love of mockery; for I know this letter will make a contemplative idiot of him. Close, in the name of jesting! Lie thou there [*throws down a letter*]; for here comes the trout that must be caught with tickling.       [*Exit.*

*Enter* MALVOLIO.

MALVOLIO.

'Tis but fortune; all is fortune. Maria once told me she did affect[3] me: and I have heard herself come thus near, that, should she fancy, it should be one of my complexion.[4] Be-

---

[1] sheep-biter: a dog that bites sheep; hence, a petty thief.
[2] metal of India: precious metal; gold.
[3] affect: favor.
[4] complexion: disposition; nature.

sides, she uses me with a more exalted respect than any one else that follows her. What should I think on't?

SIR TOBY BELCH.

Here's an overweening rogue!

FABIAN.

O, peace! Contemplation makes a rare turkey-cock of him: how he jets[1] under his advanced plumes!

SIR ANDREW AGUECHEEK.

'Slight,[2] I could so beat the rogue!

SIR TOBY BELCH.

Peace, I say.

MALVOLIO.

To be Count Malvolio,—

SIR TOBY BELCH.

Ah, rogue!

SIR ANDREW AGUECHEEK.

Pistol him, pistol him.

SIR TOBY BELCH.

Peace, peace!

MALVOLIO.

There is example for't; the lady of the Strachy married the yeoman of the wardrobe.

SIR ANDREW AGUECHEEK.

Fie on him, Jezebel![3]

FABIAN.

O, peace! now he's deeply in: look how imagination blows him.[4]

MALVOLIO.

Having been three months married to her, sitting in my state,[5]—

SIR TOBY BELCH.

O, for a stone-bow, to hit him in the eye!

---

[1] jets: struts.
[2] 'Slight: "God's light."
[3] Jezebel: wife of Ahab, king of Israel, known for her wickedness.
[4] blows him: puffs him up.
[5] state: position; chair of state.

MALVOLIO.

Calling my officers about me, in my brancht velvet gown;
having come from a day-bed, where I have left Olivia sleep-
ing,—

SIR TOBY BELCH.

Fire and brimstone!

FABIAN.

O, peace, peace!

MALVOLIO.

And then to have the humour of state;[1] and after a demure
travel of regard,[2]—telling them I know my place, as I would
they should do theirs,—to ask for my kinsman Toby,—

SIR TOBY BELCH.

Bolts and shackles!

FABIAN.

O, peace, peace, peace! now, now.

MALVOLIO.

Seven of my people, with an obedient start, make out for
him:[3] I frown the while; and perchance wind up my watch,
or play with some rich jewel. Toby approaches; court'sies
there to me,—

SIR TOBY BELCH.

Shall this fellow live?

FABIAN.

Though our silence be drawn from us with cars, yet peace.

MALVOLIO.

I extend my hand to him thus, quenching my familiar smile
with an austere regard of control,[4]—

SIR TOBY BELCH.

And does not Toby take you[5] a blow o'the lips, then?

---

[1] humour of state: express by action the dignity of office.
[2] demure/travel of regard: casual survey of the assembly.
[3] make out for/him: go to look for him.
[4] austere regard of control: a stern, authoritative look.
[5] take: give.

MALVOLIO.

Saying, 'Cousin Toby, my fortunes having cast me on your niece, give me this prerogative of speech,'—

SIR TOBY BELCH.

What, what?

MALVOLIO.

'You must amend your drunkenness.'

SIR TOBY BELCH.

Out, scab! [1]

FABIAN.

Nay, patience, or we break the sinews of our plot. [2]

MALVOLIO.

'Besides, you waste the treasure of your time with a foolish knight,'—

SIR ANDREW AGUECHEEK.

That's me, I warrant you.

MALVOLIO.

'One Sir Andrew,'—

SIR ANDREW AGUECHEEK.

I knew 'twas I; for many do call me fool.

MALVOLIO.

What employment have we here?      [*Taking up the letter.*

FABIAN.

Now is the woodcock near the gin. [3]

SIR TOBY BELCH.

O, peace! and the spirit of humours [4] intimate reading aloud to him!

MALVOLIO.

By my life, this is my lady's hand: these be her very C's, her U's, and her T's; and thus makes she her great P's. It is, in contempt of question, her hand.

SIR ANDREW AGUECHEEK.

Her C's, her U's, and her T's: why that?

---

[1] scab: scurvy (fellow).
[2] break the sinews of our plot: weaken our scheme.
[3] gin: snare.
[4] spirit of humours: the mover of impulses.

MALVOLIO [*reads*].

To the unknown beloved, this, and my good wishes: her very phrases!—By your leave, wax.[1]—Soft! [2]—and the impressure her Lucrece, with which she uses to seal: 'tis my lady. To whom should this be?

FABIAN.

This wins him, liver and all.

MALVOLIO [*reads*].

> Jove knows I love:
>      But who?
> Lips, do not move;
> No man must know.

'No man must know.'—What follows? the numbers alter'd!—'No man must know:'—if this should be thee, Malvolio?

SIR TOBY BELCH.

Marry,[3] hang thee, brock![4]

MALVOLIO [*reads*].

> I may command where I adore;
>      But silence, like a Lucrece knife,[5]
> With bloodless stroke my heart doth gore:
>      M, O, A, I, doth sway my life.

FABIAN.

A fustian riddle! [6]

SIR TOBY BELCH.

Excellent wench, say I.

MALVOLIO.

'M, O, A, I, doth sway my life.'—Nay, but first, let me see, —let me see,—let me see.

---

[1] wax: seal.
[2] soft: easy; carefully.
[3] Marry: by the Virgin Mary.
[4] brock: badger (foul-smelling); a term of abuse.
[5] Lucrece knife: suicidal knife.
[6] fustian riddle: claptrap.

FABIAN.

What dish o'poison has she drest[1] him!

SIR TOBY BELCH.

And with what wing the staniel checks[2] at it!

MALVOLIO.

'I may command where I adore.' Why, she may command me: I serve her; she is my lady. Why, this is evident to any formal capacity;[3] there is no obstruction in this:—and the end,—what should that alphabetical position portend? if I could make that resemble something in me,—Softly!—M, O, A, I,—

SIR TOBY BELCH.

O, ay, make up that:—he is now at a cold scent.

FABIAN.

Sowter[4] will cry upon't,[5] for all this, though it be as rank as a fox.

MALVOLIO.

M,—Malvolio;—M,—why, that begins my name.

FABIAN.

Did not I say he would work it out? the cur is excellent at faults.[6]

MALVOLIO.

M,—but then there is no consonancy[7] in the sequel; that suffers under probation:[8] A should follow, but O does.

FABIAN.

And O shall end, I hope.

SIR TOBY BELCH.

Ay, or I'll cudgel him, and make him cry O!

MALVOLIO.

And then I comes behind.

---

[1] drest: stuffed; prepared. [2] staniel checks: the hawk pursues a false quarry. [3] formal capacity: normal understanding. [4] Sowter: a bungler. [5] cry upon't: take up the chase. [6] faults: a hunting term, forsaking quarry for a false scent. [7] consonancy: consistency. [8] suffers under probation: cannot stand close scrutiny.

**FABIAN.**

Ay, an you had any eye behind you, you might see more detraction at your heels than fortunes before you.

**MALVOLIO.**

M, O, A, I;—this simulation is not as the former:—and yet, to crush this a little,[1] it would bow to me,[2] for every one of these letters are in my name. Soft! here follows prose.— [reads] If this fall into thy hand, revolve.[3] In my stars[4] I am above thee; but be not afraid of greatness: some are born great, some achieve greatness, and some have greatness thrust upon 'em. Thy Fates open their hands; let thy blood and spirit embrace them: and, to inure thyself to what thou art like to be, cast thy humble slough,[5] and appear fresh. Be opposite with a kinsman, surly with servants; let thy tongue tang arguments of state;[6] put thyself into the trick of singularity;[7] she thus advises thee that sighs for thee. Remember who commended thy yellow stockings, and wisht to see thee ever cross-garter'd: I say, remember. Go to, thou art made, if thou desirest to be so; if not, let me see thee a steward still, the fellow of servants, and not worthy to touch Fortune's fingers. Farewell. She that would alter services[8] with thee,

THE FORTUNATE-UNHAPPY.

Daylight and champain[9] discovers not more: this is open. I will be proud, I will read politic authors, I will baffle Sir Toby, I will wash off gross acquaintance, I will be point-devise the very man.[10] I do not now fool myself, to let imagination jade[11] me; for every reason excites to this,[12] that

---

[1] to crush this a little: with a little persuasion. [2] it would bow to me: it will reveal its meaning to me. [3] revolve: consider. [4] stars: destiny. [5] humble slough: ragged clothes. [6] tang arguments of state: discuss matters of state. [7] singu/larity: individuality. [8] alter services: exchange roles; become subordinate. [9] champain: open expanse. [10] point-/devise the very man: the perfect man in every way. [11] jade: trick. [12] excites to this: points to this.

my lady loves me. She did commend my yellow stockings of late, she did praise my leg being cross-garter'd; and in this she manifests herself to my love, and, with a kind of injunction, drives me to these habits[1] of her liking. I thank my stars, I am happy.[2] I will be strange,[3] stout,[4] in yellow stockings, and cross-garter'd, even with the swiftness of putting on. Jove and my stars be praised!—Here is yet a postscript. [*reads*] 'Thou canst not choose but know who I am. If thou entertain'st my love, let it appear in thy smiling: thy smiles become thee well; therefore in my presence still smile, dear my sweet, I prithee.' Jove, I thank thee.—I will smile; I will do every thing that thou wilt have me.        [*Exit.*

FABIAN.
I will not give my part of this sport for a pension of thousands to be paid from the Sophy.[5]

SIR TOBY BELCH.
I could marry this wench for this device,—

SIR ANDREW AGUECHEEK.
So could I too.

SIR TOBY BELCH.
And ask no other dowry with her but such another jest.

SIR ANDREW AGUECHEEK.
Nor I neither.

FABIAN.
Here comes my noble gull-catcher.[6]

*Enter* MARIA.

SIR TOBY BELCH.
Wilt thou set thy foot o'my neck?

---

[1] **habits**: clothes.
[2] **happy**: lucky.
[3] **strange**: uncommon; reserved.
[4] **stout**: proud.
[5] **Sophy**: Shah of Persia (Iran).
[6] **gull-catcher**: fool-catcher.

**SIR ANDREW AGUECHEEK.**

Or o'mine either?

**SIR TOBY BELCH.**

Shall I play my freedom at tray-trip,[1] and become thy bond-slave?

**SIR ANDREW AGUECHEEK.**

I'faith, or I either?

**SIR TOBY BELCH.**

Why, thou hast put him in such a dream, that, when the image of it leaves him, he must run mad.

**MARIA.**

Nay, but say true; does it work upon him?

**SIR TOBY BELCH.**

Like aqua-vitæ[2] with a midwife.

**MARIA.**

If you will then see the fruits of the sport, mark his first approach before my lady: he will come to her in yellow stockings, and 'tis a colour she abhors, and cross-garter'd, a fashion she detests; and he will smile upon her, which will now be so unsuitable to her disposition, being addicted to a melancholy as she is, that it cannot but turn him into a notable contempt. If you will see it, follow me.

**SIR TOBY BELCH.**

To the gates of Tartar,[3] thou most excellent devil of wit!

**SIR ANDREW AGUECHEEK.**

I'll make one[4] too.                    [*Exeunt.*

---

[1] **tray-trip:** dice game.
[2] **aqua-vitæ:** brandy; strong liquor; literally, "water of life."
[3] **gates of Tartar:** gates of Tartarus; the infernal regions of ancient mythology.
[4] **make one:** go along.

# Twelfth Night

## ACT 3

# ACT III

Viola on her way to the Countess meets first the Clown,
Sir Toby, and Sir Andrew; then Olivia appears, greeting Viola
(Cesario) with such warmth as to annoy Sir Andrew, who
still hopes to win the Countess's love. After they leave, Olivia
openly declares her love for the young page, who must, of
course, reject it as graciously as he (she) can. But Sir Toby
and Fabian (Olivia's servant) trick Sir Andrew into believing
that Olivia's apparent affection for Cesario has been designed
to rouse the timid knight to action, and he decides to challenge the page to a duel. Elsewhere in town, Antonio and
Sebastian have met again, and as they part Antonio gives
Sebastian his purse, asking him to meet him at the Elephant
inn. Back at the Countess's the climax of the Malvolio plot
is reached when he appears, simpering, in yellow hose and
cross-gartered, before Olivia, who thinks he has gone mad.
Sir Toby and Maria take him off to be shut up in a dark
room—the usual treatment for madness in those days. Sir
Andrew now appears with his letter of challenge to Cesario,
which Sir Toby promises to deliver, but instead issues the
challenge orally, adding an imaginary account of Sir Andrew's
prowess. Frightened, Viola asks Sir Toby to intercede. She
leaves, and when Sir Andrew appears Sir Toby plays the
same trick on him, describing Viola as a veritable virago.
When presently knight and page come face to face for the
duel, each is terrified of the other. But as they draw swords,
Antonio, mistaking Viola for Sebastian, whose dress she has
imitated and whom she closely resembles, rushes in to protect
his supposed friend. At the same time, officers arrive and
arrest Antonio, who, as he leaves, asks for the purse he has
lent Sebastian. Viola, of course, knows nothing of it, and her
bewilderment appearing like cowardice causes Sir Andrew to
gain fresh courage and he sets off after her to continue the
duel.

# ACT III. Scene I.

### OLIVIA's garden.

*Enter* VIOLA, *and* CLOWN *with a tabor.*

**VIOLA.**

Save thee, friend, and thy music! dost thou live by thy tabor? [1]

**CLOWN.**

No, sir, I live by the church.

**VIOLA.**

Art thou a churchman?

**CLOWN.**

No such matter, sir: I do live by the church; for I do live at my house, and my house doth stand by the church.

**VIOLA.**

So thou mayst say, the king lies by a beggar, if a beggar dwell near him; or, the church stands by thy tabor, if thy tabor stand by the church.

**CLOWN.**

You have said, sir.—To see this age!—A sentence is but a cheveril [2] glove to a good wit: how quickly the wrong side may be turn'd outward!

**VIOLA.**

Nay, that's certain; they that dally [3] nicely with words may quickly make them wanton.

**CLOWN.**

I would, therefore, my sister had had no name, sir.

**VIOLA.**

Why, man?

**CLOWN.**

Why, sir, her name's a word; and to dally with that word might make my sister wanton. But, indeed, words are very rascals, since bonds disgraced them. [4]

---

[1] tabor: drum.

[2] cheveril: kidskin; very soft leather.

[3] dally: play.

[4] words are very/rascals, since bonds disgraced them: having to put up a bond for them makes words no longer good.

**VIOLA.**

Thy reason, man?

**CLOWN.**

Troth, sir, I can yield you none without words; and words are
grown so false, I am loth to prove reason with them.

**VIOLA.**

I warrant thou art a merry fellow, and carest for nothing.

**CLOWN.**

Not so, sir; I do care for something; but in my conscience,
sir, I do not care for you: if that be to care for nothing, sir,
I would it would make you invisible.

**VIOLA.**

Art not thou the Lady Olivia's fool?

**CLOWN.**

No, indeed, sir; the Lady Olivia has no folly: she will keep
no fool, sir, till she be married; and fools are as like husbands
as pilchers[1] are to herrings,—the husband's the bigger: I am,
indeed, not her fool, but her corrupter of words.

**VIOLA.**

I saw thee late[2] at the Count Orsino's.

**CLOWN.**

Foolery, sir, does walk about the orb[3] like the sun, it shines
every where. I would be sorry, sir, but the fool should be as
oft with your master as with my mistress: I think I saw your
wisdom there.

**VIOLA.**

Nay, an thou pass upon me,[4] I'll no more with thee. Hold,
there's expenses for thee.

---

[1] pilchers: a herringlike fish (pilchards).
[2] late: recently.
[3] orb: the earth.
[4] pass upon me: make verbal sport of me ("pass" is a term in
dueling).

CLOWN.

Now Jove, in his next commodity[1] of hair, send thee a beard!

VIOLA.

By my troth, I'll tell thee, I am almost sick for one;[2] though I would not have it grow on my chin. Is thy lady within?

CLOWN.

Would not a pair of these have bred, sir?

VIOLA.

Yes, being kept together and put to use.

CLOWN.

I would play Lord Pandarus[3] of Phrygia, sir, to bring a Cressida to this Troilus.

VIOLA.

I understand you, sir; 'tis well begg'd.

CLOWN.

The matter, I hope,. is not great, sir, begging but a beggar: Cressida was a beggar. My lady is within, sir. I will conster[4] to them whence you come; who you are, and what you would, are out of my welkin,—I might say element, but the word is over-worn.                                                      [*Exit.*

VIOLA.

This fellow is wise enough to play the fool;
And to do that well craves[5] a kind of wit:
He must observe their mood on whom he jests,
The quality of persons, and the time;
Not, like the haggard,[6] check at[7] every feather
That comes before his eye. This is a practice
As full of labour as a wise man's art:
For folly, that he wisely shows, is fit;[8]
But wise men, folly-fall'n, quite taint their wit.

---

[1] commodity: parcel of goods. [2] sick for one: sick for sight of one special beard. [3] Pandarus: leader of the Lycians in the Trojan war, who conspired to procure Cressida, his niece, for Troilus, son of Priam. [4] conster: construe. [5] craves: calls for. [6] haggard: wild hawk. [7] check at: chase. [8] fit: suitable.

*Enter* SIR TOBY *and* SIR ANDREW.

SIR TOBY BELCH.

Save you,[1] gentleman!

VIOLA.

And you, sir.

SIR ANDREW AGUECHEEK.

*Dieu vous garde, monsieur.*[2]

VIOLA.

*Et vous aussi; votre serviteur.*[3]

SIR ANDREW AGUECHEEK.

I hope, sir, you are; and I am yours.

SIR TOBY BELCH.

Will you encounter[4] the house? my niece is desirous you should enter, if your trade be to her.[5]

VIOLA.

I am bound to your niece, sir; I mean, she is the list[6] of my voyage.

SIR TOBY BELCH.

Taste your legs, sir; put them to motion.

VIOLA.

My legs do better understand me, sir, than I understand what you mean by bidding me taste my legs.

SIR TOBY BELCH.

I mean, to go, sir, to enter.

VIOLA.

I will answer you with gait and entrance:—but we are prevented.

*Enter* OLIVIA *and* MARIA.

Most excellent accomplisht lady, the heavens rain odours on you!

SIR ANDREW AGUECHEEK [*aside*].

That youth's a rare courtier: 'Rain odours:'—well.

---

[1] Save you: God save you.

[2] *Dieu vous gard, monsieur:* God save you, sir.

[3] *Et vous aussi; votre serviteur:* and you also; your servant.

[4] encounter: go to; literally, to confront.

[5] if your trade be to her: if your business concerns her.

[6] list: end.

VIOLA.

My matter hath no voice, lady, but to your own most pregnant and vouchsafed [1] ear.

SIR ANDREW AGUECHEEK [aside].

'Odours,' 'pregnant,' and 'vouchsafed':—I'll get 'em all three all ready.

OLIVIA.

Let the garden-door be shut, and leave me to my hearing. [Exeunt SIR TOBY, SIR ANDREW, and MARIA.] Give me your hand, sir.

VIOLA.

My duty, madam, and most humble service.

OLIVIA.

What is your name?

VIOLA.

Cesario is your servant's name, fair princess.

OLIVIA.

My servant, sir! 'Twas never merry world
Since lowly feigning[2] was call'd compliment:
Y'are servant to the Count Orsino, youth.

VIOLA.

And he is yours, and his must needs be yours:
Your servant's servant is your servant, madam.

OLIVIA.

For him, I think not on him: for his thoughts,
Would they were blanks, rather than fill'd with me!

VIOLA.

Madam, I come to whet your gentle thoughts
On his behalf:—

OLIVIA.

O, by your leave, I pray you,—
I bade you never speak again of him:

---

[1] preg/nant and vouchsafed: ready and accommodating.
[2] lowly feigning: feigned humbleness.

But, would you undertake another suit,
I had rather hear you to solicit that
Than music from the spheres.[1]

VIOLA.

                            Dear lady,—

OLIVIA.

Give me leave, beseech you. I did send,
After the last enchantment you did here,
A ring in chase of you: so did I abuse[2]
Myself, my servant, and, I fear me, you:
Under your hard construction[3] must I sit,
To force that on you, in a shameful cunning,
Which you knew none of yours: what might you think?
Have you not set mine honour at the stake,
And baited it with all th'unmuzzled thoughts
That tyrannous heart can think? To one of your receiving
Enough is shown: a cypress,[4] not a bosom,
Hides my poor heart. So, let me hear you speak.

VIOLA.

I pity you.

OLIVIA.

            That's a degree[5] to love.

VIOLA.

No, not a grise;[6] for 'tis a vulgar proof,[7]
That very oft we pity enemies.

OLIVIA.

Why, then, methinks 'tis time to smile again.
O world, how apt the poor are to be proud!
If one should be a prey, how much the better
To fall before the lion than the wolf! [8]            [*Clock strikes.*

---

[1] spheres: heavens. [2] abuse: fool; deceive. [3] hard construction: low
opinion. [4] cypress: fine silk gauze from the island of Cypress,
usually dyed black and used in mourning. [5] degree: stage. [6] grise:
also degree. [7] vulgar proof: common knowledge. [8] To fall before
the lion than the wolf!: to give her heart to someone noble and
strong rather than to someone inferior and cruel.

The clock upbraids me with the waste of time.—
Be not afraid, good youth, I will not have you:
And yet, when wit and youth is come to harvest,[1]
Your wife is like to reap a proper man:
There lies your way, due west.[2]

     VIOLA.

                    Then westward-ho!—
Grace and good disposition attend your ladyship!
You'll nothing,[3] madam, to my lord by me?

     OLIVIA.

Stay:
I prithee, tell me what thou think'st of me.

     VIOLA.

That you do think you are not what you are.

     OLIVIA.

If I think so, I think the same of you.

     VIOLA.

Then think you right: I am not what I am.

     OLIVIA.

I would you were as I would have you be!

     VIOLA.

Would it be better, madam, than I am,
I wish it might; for now I am your fool.

     OLIVIA.

O, what a deal of scorn looks beautiful
In the contempt and anger of his lip!
A murderous guilt shows not itself more soon
Than love that would seem hid: love's night is noon.[4]
Cesario, by the roses of the spring,
By maidhood, honour, truth, and every thing,
I love thee so, that, maugre[5] all thy pride,
Nor wit nor reason can my passion hide.

---

[1] come to harvest: mature; adulthood.
[2] due west: clear course.
[3] You'll nothing: you'll send no message.
[4] love's night is noon: love's passion is undimmed by night; nothing can hide it.
[5] maugre: notwithstanding.

Do not extort thy reasons from this clause,
For that I woo, thou therefore hast no cause;
But, rather, reason thus with reason fetter,—
Love sought is good, but given unsought is better.

VIOLA.

By innocence I swear, and by my youth,
I have one heart, one bosom, and one truth,—
And that no woman has; nor never none
Shall mistress be of it, save I alone.
And so adieu, good madam: never more
Will I my master's tears to you deplore.

OLIVIA.

Yet come again; for thou perhaps mayst move
That heart, which now abhors, to like his love. [*Exeunt.*

## SCENE II.

OLIVIA's *house.*

*Enter* SIR TOBY, SIR ANDREW, *and* FABIAN.

SIR ANDREW AGUECHEEK.

No, faith, I'll not stay a jot longer.

SIR TOBY BELCH.

Thy reason, dear venom; give thy reason.

FABIAN.

You must needs yield your reason, Sir Andrew.

SIR ANDREW AGUECHEEK.

Marry, I saw your niece do more favours to the count's
serving-man than ever she bestow'd upon me; I saw't
i'th'orchard.

SIR TOBY BELCH.

Did she see thee the while, old boy? tell me that.

SIR ANDREW AGUECHEEK.

As plain as I see you now.

FABIAN.

This was a great argument of love in her toward you.

SIR ANDREW AGUECHEEK.

'Slight, will you make an ass o'me?

FABIAN.

I will prove it legitimate, sir, upon the oaths of judgement and reason.

SIR TOBY BELCH.

And they have been grand-jurymen since before Noah was a sailor.

FABIAN.

She did show favour to the youth in your sight only to exasperate you, to awake your dormouse valour, to put fire in your heart, and brimstone in your liver. You should then have accosted her; and with some excellent jests, fire-new from the mint, you should have bang'd [1] the youth into dumbness. This was lookt for at your hand, and this was balkt: [2] the double gilt of this opportunity you let time wash off, and you are now sail'd into the north of my lady's opinion; where you will hang like an icicle on a Dutchman's beard, unless you do redeem it by some laudable attempt either of valour or policy.

SIR ANDREW AGUECHEEK.

An't be any way, it must be with valour; for policy [3] I hate: I had as lief be a Brownist [4] as a politician.

SIR TOBY BELCH.

Why, then, build me thy fortunes upon the basis of valour. Challenge me the count's youth to fight with him; hurt him

---

[1] bang'd: beat.
[2] balkt: passed over; ignored.
[3] policy: stratagem or trick.
[4] Brownist: a follower of Robert Brown, an English divine and a leader among the early Separatist Puritans; he formulated the principles of Congregationalism.

in eleven places: my niece shall take note of it; and assure
thyself, there is no love-broker in the world can more prevail
in man's commendation with woman than report of valour.

FABIAN.

There is no way but this, Sir Andrew.

SIR ANDREW AGUECHEEK.

Will either of you bear me a challenge to him?

SIR TOBY BELCH.

Go, write it in a martial hand; be curst[1] and brief; it is no
matter how witty, so it be eloquent and full of invention:
taunt him with the license of ink:[2] if thou 'thou'st' him some
thrice, it shall not be amiss; and as many lies as will lie in
thy sheet of paper, although the sheet were big enough for
the bed of Ware[3] in England, set 'em down: go, about it.
Let there be gall enough in thy ink, though thou write with
a goose-pen, no matter: about it.

SIR ANDREW AGUECHEEK.

Where shall I find you?

SIR TOBY BELCH.

We'll call thee at the *cubiculo:*[4] go.        [*Exit* SIR ANDREW.

FABIAN.

This is a dear manakin[5] to you, Sir Toby.

SIR TOBY BELCH.

I have been dear[6] to him, lad,—some two thousand strong,
or so.

FABIAN.

We shall have a rare letter from him: but you'll not deliver't?

---

[1] curst: sharp.
[2] license of ink: write freely.
[3] bed of Ware: a very large four-poster bed.
[4] *cubiculo:* bedroom or chamber (cubicle).
[5] manakin: plaything.
[6] dear: costly.

SIR TOBY BELCH.

Never trust me, then; and by all means stir on the youth to
an answer. I think oxen and wainropes[1] cannot hale[2] them
together. For Andrew, if he were open'd, and you find so
much blood in his liver[3] as will clog the foot of a flea, I'll eat
the rest of th'anatomy.

FABIAN.

And his opposite,[4] the youth, bears in his visage no great
presage of cruelty.

SIR TOBY BELCH.

Look, where the youngest wren of nine comes.

*Enter* MARIA.

MARIA.

If you desire the spleen, and will laugh yourselves into
stitches, follow me. Yond gull [5] Malvolio is turn'd heathen,
a very renegado;[6] for there is no Christian, that means to be
saved by believing rightly, can ever believe such impossible
passages of grossness. He's in yellow stockings.

SIR TOBY BELCH.

And cross-garter'd?

MARIA.

Most villainously; like a pedant that keeps a school i'th'church.
—I have dogg'd him, like his murderer. He does obey every
point of the letter that I dropt to betray him: he does smile
his face into more lines than is in the new map, with the
augmentation of the Indies: you have not seen such a thing
as 'tis; I can hardly forbear hurling things at him. I know my
lady will strike him: if she do, he'll smile, and take't for a
great favour.

SIR TOBY BELCH.

Come, bring us, bring us where he is.                    [*Exeunt.*

---

[1] wainropes: strong wagon ropes.
[2] hale: hold.
[3] blood in his liver: courage.
[4] opposite: adversary.
[5] gull: fool.
[6] renegado: renegade.

## SCENE III.

### A street.

### Enter SEBASTIAN and ANTONIO.

SEBASTIAN.

I would not, by my will, have troubled you;
But, since you make your pleasure of your pains,
I will no further chide you.

ANTONIO.

I could not stay behind you: my desire,
More sharp than filed steel, did spur me forth;
And not all love to see you,—though so much
As might have drawn me to a longer voyage,—
But jealousy[1] what might befall your travel,
Being skilless in these parts; which to a stranger,
Unguided and unfriended, often prove
Rough and unhospitable: my willing love,
The rather by these arguments of fear,
Set forth in your pursuit.

SEBASTIAN.

           My kind Antonio,
I can no other answer make, but thanks,
And thanks, and ever; oft good turns
Are shuffled off with such uncurrent[2] pay:
But, were my worth, as is my conscience, firm,
You should find better dealing. What's to do?
Shall we go see the reliques[3] of this town?

ANTONIO.

To-morrow, sir; best first go see your lodging.

SEBASTIAN.

I am not weary, and 'tis long to night:
I pray you, let us satisfy our eyes
With the memorials and the things of fame

---

[1] jealousy: apprehension.
[2] uncurrent: not full value.
[3] reliques: archaic form of "relics"; monuments; memorials.

That do renown[1] this city.

ANTONIO.

                                 Would you'ld pardon me;
I do not without danger walk these streets:
Once, in a sea-fight, 'gainst the count his galleys
I did some service; of such note, indeed,
That, were I ta'en here, it would scarce be answer'd.[2]

SEBASTIAN.

Belike you slew great number of his people?

ANTONIO.

Th'offence is not of such a bloody nature;
Albeit the quality of the time and quarrel
Might well have given us bloody argument.
It might have since been answer'd in repaying
What we took from them; which, for traffic's[3] sake,
Most of our city did: only myself stood out;
For which, if I be lapsed [4] in this place,
I shall pay dear.

SEBASTIAN.

                           Do not, then, walk too open.

ANTONIO.

It doth not fit me. Hold, sir, here's my purse.
In the south suburbs, at the Elephant,
Is best to lodge: I will bespeak our diet,[5]
Whiles you beguile the time and feed your knowledge
With viewing of the town: there shall you have me.[6]

SEBASTIAN.

Why I your purse?

ANTONIO.

Hap'y[7] your eye shall light upon some toy
You have desire to purchase; and your store,[8]
I think, is not for idle markets,[9] sir.

---

[1] renown: make famous. [2] it would scarce be answer'd: it would
be difficult to explain his previous actions. [3] traffic: trade; commerce. [4] lapsed: apprehended; taken. [5] bespeak our diet: order our
food. [6] have me: find me. [7] hap'y: haply. [8] store: money. [9] idle
markets: free and loose buying.

SEBASTIAN.

I'll be your purse-bearer, and leave you for
An hour.

ANTONIO.

       To th'Elephant.

SEBASTIAN.

                 I do remember.          [*Exeunt.*

## SCENE IV.

### OLIVIA's *garden.*

#### Enter OLIVIA *and* MARIA.

OLIVIA.

I have sent after him: he says he'll come;—
How shall I feast him? what bestow of him?
For youth is bought more oft than begg'd or borrow'd.
I speak too loud.—
Where is Malvolio?—he is sad and civil,[1]
And suits well for a servant with my fortunes:—
Where is Malvolio?

MARIA.

He's coming, madam; but in very strange manner. He is, sure,
possest, madam.

OLIVIA.

Why, what's the matter? does he rave?

MARIA.

No, madam, he does nothing but smile: your ladyship were
best to have some guard about you, if he come; for, sure, the
man is tainted in's[2] wits.

OLIVIA.

Go call him hither. [*Exit* MARIA.] I am as mad as he,
If sad and merry madness equal be.

---

[1] sad and civil: serious and polite.
[2] in's: in his.

*Enter* MARIA, *with* MALVOLIO.

How now, Malvolio!
> MALVOLIO.

Sweet lady, ho, ho.                              [*Smiles fantastically.*
> OLIVIA.

Smilest thou?
I sent for thee upon a sad occasion.[1]
> MALVOLIO.

Sad, lady! I could be sad: this does make some obstruction
in the blood, this cross-gartering; but what of that? if it
please the eye of one, it is with me as the very true sonnet is,
'Please one, and please all.'
> OLIVIA.

Why, how dost thou, man? what is the matter with thee?
> MALVOLIO.

Not black in my mind, though yellow in my legs. It did come
to his hands, and commands shall be executed: I think we do
know the sweet Roman hand.[2]
> OLIVIA.

Wilt thou go to bed, Malvolio?
> MALVOLIO.

To bed! ay, sweet-heart; and I'll come to thee.
> OLIVIA.

God comfort thee! Why dost thou smile so, and kiss thy
hand so oft?
> MARIA.

How do you, Malvolio?
> MALVOLIO.

At your request! yes: nightingales answer daws.[3]

---

[1] sad occasion: serious matter.
[2] hand: handwriting.
[3] daws: jackdaws.

MARIA.

Why appear you with this ridiculous boldness before my lady?

MALVOLIO.

'Be not afraid of greatness:'—'twas well writ.

OLIVIA.

What mean'st thou by that, Malvolio?

MALVOLIO.

'Some are born great,'—

OLIVIA.

Ha!

MALVOLIO.

'Some achieve greatness,'—

OLIVIA.

What say'st thou?

MALVOLIO.

'And some have greatness thrust upon them.'

OLIVIA.

Heaven restore thee!

MALVOLIO.

'Remember who commended thy yellow stockings,'—

OLIVIA.

Thy yellow stockings!

MALVOLIO.

'And wisht to see thee cross-garter'd.'

OLIVIA.

Cross-garter'd!

MALVOLIO.

Go to, thou art made, if thou desirest to be so;'—

OLIVIA.

Am I made?

MALVOLIO.

'If not, let me see thee a servant still.'

OLIVIA.

Why, this is very midsummer madness.

*Enter a* SERVANT.

SERVANT.

Madam, the young gentleman of the Count Orsino's is return'd: I could hardly entreat him back: he attends your
ladyship's pleasure.

OLIVIA.

I'll come to him. [*Exit* SERVANT.] Good Maria, let this fellow
be lookt to. Where's my cousin Toby? Let some of my people
have a special care of him: I would not have him miscarry[1]
for the half of my dowry.          [*Exeunt* OLIVIA *and* MARIA.

MALVOLIO.

O, ho! do you come near me[2] now? no worse man than Sir
Toby to look to me? This concurs directly with the letter:
she sends him on purpose, that I may appear stubborn[3] to
him; for she incites me to that in the letter. 'Cast thy humble
slough,' says she; 'be opposite with a kinsman, surly with
servants; let thy tongue tang with arguments of state; put
thyself into the trick of singularity;'—and, consequently, sets
down the manner how; as, a sad face, a reverend carriage, a
slow tongue, in the habit of some sir of note, and so forth.
I have limed[4] her; but it is Joves's doing, and Jove make me
thankful! And, when she went away now, 'Let this fellow be
lookt to:' fellow! not Malvolio, nor after my degree,[5] but
fellow. Why, every thing adheres together, that no dram of a
scruple,[6] no scruple of a scruple, no obstacle, no incredulous
or unsafe circumstance—What can be said? Nothing, that

---

[1] miscarry: be lost; come to grief. [2] come near me: see things as I
do. [3] stubborn: firm. [4] limed: ensnared; to entangle as with bird-
lime. [5] degree: station. [6] no dram of a/scruple: both dram and
scruple imply small amount; hence, no slightest thing.

can be, can come between me and the full prospect of my
hopes. Well, Jove, not I, is the doer of this, and he is to be
thankt.

*Enter* MARIA *with* SIR TOBY *and* FABIAN.

SIR TOBY BELCH.

Which way is he, in the name of sanctity? If all the devils of
hell be drawn in little, and Legion himself possest him,[1] yet
I'll speak to him.

FABIAN.

Here he is, here he is.—How is't with you, sir? how is't with
you, man?

MALVOLIO.

Go off; I discard you: let me enjoy my private:[2] go off.

MARIA.

Lo, how hollow the fiend speaks within him; did not I tell
you?—Sir Toby, my lady prays you to have a care of him.

MALVOLIO.

Ah, ha! does she so?

SIR TOBY BELCH.

Go to, go to; peace, peace; we must deal gently with him:
let me alone.—How do you, Malvolio? how is't with you?
What, man! defy the devil: consider, he's an enemy to mankind.

MALVOLIO.

Do you know what you say?

MARIA.

La you, an you speak ill of the devil, how he takes it at heart!
Pray God, he be not bewitcht!

FABIAN.

Carry his water to th'wise woman.[3]

---

[1] **Legion himself possest him:** possessed of many devils (a Biblical
allusion).
[2] **private:** privacy.
[3] **Carry his water to the wise woman:** go to a witch for advice:
literally, for urinalysis.

MARIA.

Marry, and it shall be done to-morrow morning, if I live. My lady would not lose him for more than I'll say.

MALVOLIO.

How now, mistress!

MARIA.

O Lord!

SIR TOBY BELCH.

Prithee, hold thy peace; this is not the way: do you not see you move him? let me alone with him.

FABIAN.

No way but gentleness; gently, gently: the fiend is rough, and will not be roughly used.

SIR TOBY BELCH.

Why, how now, my bawcock! [1] how dost thou, chuck? [2]

MALVOLIO.

Sir!

SIR TOBY BELCH.

Ay, Biddy,[3] come with me. What, man! 'tis not for gravity to play at cherry-pit[4] with Satan: hang him, foul collier! [5]

MARIA.

Get him to say his prayers; good Sir Toby, get him to pray.

MALVOLIO.

My prayers, minx!

MARIA.

No, I warrant you, he will not hear of godliness.

MALVOLIO.

Go, hang yourselves all! you are idle shallow things: I am not of your element:[6] you shall know more hereafter.   [Exit.

---

[1] bawcock: fine fellow.
[2] chuck: chicken: a term of endearment.
[3] Biddy: maidservant.
[4] cherry-pit: a children's game of pitching cherry stones into a hole.
[5] foul collier: dirty coal miner.
[6] element: composition.

SIR TOBY BELCH.

Is't possible?

FABIAN.

If this were play'd upon a stage now, I could condemn it as an improbable fiction.

SIR TOBY BELCH.

His very genius[1] hath taken the infection of the device,[2] man.

MARIA.

Nay, pursue him now, lest the device take air, and taint.[3]

FABIAN.

Why, we shall make him mad indeed.

MARIA.

The house will be the quieter.

SIR TOBY BELCH.

Come, we'll have him in a dark room and bound. My niece is already in the belief that he's mad; we may carry it thus, for our pleasure and his penance, till our very pastime, tired out of breath, prompt us to have mercy on him: at which time we will bring the device to the bar,[4] and crown thee for a finder of madmen.—But see, but see.

FABIAN.

More matter for a May morning.

*Enter* SIR ANDREW.

SIR ANDREW AGUECHEEK.

Here's the challenge, read it: I warrant there's vinegar and pepper in't.

FABIAN.

Is't so saucy?

SIR ANDREW AGUECHEEK.

Ay, is't, I warrant him: do but read.

---

[1] genius: nature.
[2] device: scheme.
[3] take air, and taint: be exposed and, therefore, spoiled.
[4] bar: bar of justice.

SIR TOBY BELCH.

Give me. [*reads*] Youth, whatsoever thou art, thou art but a scurvy fellow.

FABIAN.

Good, and valiant.

SIR TOBY BELCH [*reads*].

Wonder not, nor admire not in thy mind, why I do call thee so, for I will show thee no reason for't.

FABIAN.

A good note: that keeps you from the blow of the law.

SIR TOBY BELCH [*reads*].

Thou comest to the Lady Olivia, and in my sight she uses thee kindly: but thou liest in thy throat; that is not the matter I challenge thee for.

FABIAN.

Very brief, and to exceeding good sense—less.

SIR TOBY BELCH [*reads*].

I will waylay thee going home; where if it be thy chance to kill me,—

FABIAN.

Good.

SIR TOBY BELCH [*reads*].

Thou kill'st me like a rogue and a villain.

FABIAN.

Still you keep o'th'windy side of the law:[1] good.

SIR TOBY BELCH [*reads*].

Fare thee well; and God have mercy upon one of our souls! He may have mercy upon mine; but my hope is better, and so look to thyself. Thy friend, as thou usest him, and thy sworn enemy,

ANDREW AGUECHEEK.

---

[1] o'th'windy side of the law: safe side of the law; out of reach; clear.

If this letter move him not, his legs cannot: I'll give't him.

MARIA.

You may have very fit occasion for't: he is now in some commerce[1] with my lady, and will by and by depart.

SIR TOBY BELCH.

Go, Sir Andrew; scout me for him at the corner of the orchard, like a bum-baily:[2] so soon as ever thou seest him, draw; and, as thou draw'st, swear horrible; for it comes to pass oft, that a terrible oath, with a swaggering accent sharply twang'd off, gives manhood more approbation[3] then ever proof [4] itself would have earn'd him. Away!

SIR ANDREW AGUECHEEK.

Nay, let me alone[5] for swearing. [*Exit.*

SIR TOBY BELCH.

Now will not I deliver his letter: for the behaviour of the young gentleman gives him out to be of good capacity and breeding: his employment between his lord and my niece confirms no less: therefore this letter, being so excellently ignorant, will breed no terror in the youth: he will find it comes from a clodpole.[6] But, sir, I will deliver his challenge by word of mouth; set upon Aguecheek a notable report of valour; and drive the gentleman—as I know his youth will aptly receive it—into a most hideous opinion of his rage, skill, fury, and impetuosity. This will so fright them both, that they will kill one another by the look, like cockatrices.[7]

FABIAN.

Here he comes with your niece: give them way till he take leave, and presently after him.

---

[1] com/merce: conversation. [2] bum-baily: bailiff. [3] approbation: proof. [4] proof: test. [5] let me alone: grant me eminence. [6] clodpole: dull, stupid fellow. [7] cockatrices: a legendary serpent that possessed a deadly glance.

SIR TOBY BELCH.

I will meditate the while upon some horrid message for a
challenge.    [*Exeunt* SIR TOBY, FABIAN, *and* MARIA.

*Enter* OLIVIA, *with* VIOLA.

OLIVIA.

I have said too much unto a heart of stone,
And laid mine honour too unchary[1] out:
There's something in me that reproves my fault;
But such a headstrong potent fault it is,
That it but mocks reproof.

VIOLA.

With the same 'haviour that your passion bears,
Goes on my master's griefs.

OLIVIA.

Here, wear this jewel for me, 'tis my picture:
Refuse it not: it hath no tongue to vex you:
And, I beseech you, come again to-morrow.
What shall you ask of me that I'll deny,
That honour saved may upon asking give?

VIOLA.

Nothing but this,—your true love for my master.

OLIVIA.

How with mine honour may I give him that
Which I have given to you?

VIOLA.

I will acquit[2] you.

OLIVIA.

Well, come again to-morrow; fare thee well:
A fiend like thee might bear my soul to hell.    [*Exit.*

---

[1] unchary: incautiously.
[2] acquit: release.

*Enter* SIR TOBY *and* FABIAN.

SIR TOBY BELCH.

Gentleman, God save thee!

VIOLA.

And you, sir.

SIR TOBY BELCH.

That defence thou hast, betake thee to't: of what nature the wrongs are thou hast done him, I know not: but thy intercepter, full of despite,[1] bloody as the hunter, attends thee at the orchard-end: dismount thy tuck,[2] be yare in thy preparation; for thy assailant is quick, skilful, and deadly.

VIOLA.

You mistake, sir; I am sure no man hath any quarrel to me: my remembrance is very free and clear from any image of offence done to any man.

SIR TOBY BELCH.

You'll find it otherwise, I assure you: therefore, if you hold your life at any price, betake you to your guard; for your opposite hath in him what youth, strength, skill, and wrath can furnish man withal.

VIOLA.

I pray you, sir, what is he?

SIR TOBY BELCH.

He is knight, dubb'd with unhatcht rapier[3] and on carpet[4] consideration; but he is a devil in private brawl: souls and bodies hath he divorced three; and his incensement at this moment is so implacable, that satisfaction can be none but by pangs of death and sepulchre: hob-nob[5] is his word; give't or take't.

---

[1] despite: malice; anger.
[2] dismount thy tuck: draw thy sword.
[3] unhatcht rapier: an ornamental sword, not drawn.
[4] carpet: effeminate; a knight who has spent his time in ease and luxury (a carpet knight).
[5] hob-nob: same meaning as give or take.

VIOLA.

I will return again into the house, and desire some conduct
of the lady. I am no fighter. I have heard of some kind of
men that put quarrels purposely on others, to taste their
valour; belike[1] this is a man of that quirk.[2]

SIR TOBY BELCH.

Sir, no; his indignation derives itself out of a very competent[3]
injury: therefore, get you on, and give him his desire. Back
you shall not to the house, unless you undertake that with
me which with as much safety you might answer him: therefore, on, or strip your sword stark naked; for meddle[4] you
must, that's certain, or forswear to wear iron[5] about you.

VIOLA.

This is as uncivil as strange. I beseech you, do me this cour-
teous office, as to know of the knight what my offence to him
is: it is something of my negligence, nothing of my purpose.

SIR TOBY BELCH.

I will do so.—Signior Fabian, stay you by this gentleman till
my return.                                            [Exit.

VIOLA.

Pray you, sir, do you know of this matter?

FABIAN.

I know the knight is incensed against you, even to a mortal
arbitrement;[6] but nothing of the circumstance more.

VIOLA.

I beseech you, what manner of man is he?

FABIAN.

Nothing of that wonderful promise, to read him by his form,
as you are like to find him in the proof of his valour. He is,

---

[1] belike: most likely; probably.
[2] quirk: peculiarity of behavior.
[3] competent: real.
[4] meddle: be involved.
[5] wear iron: bear arms.
[6] mortal/arbitrement: fatal decision; fight to the finish.

indeed, sir, the most skilful, bloody, and fatal opposite that you could possibly have found in any part of Illyria. Will you walk towards him? I will make your peace with him, if I can.

VIOLA.

I shall be much bound to you for't: I am one that had rather go with sir priest than sir knight: I care not who knows so much of my mettle.                    [*Exeunt.*

*Enter* SIR TOBY *and* SIR ANDREW.

SIR TOBY BELCH.

Why, man, he's a very devil; I have not seen such a firago.[1] I had a pass with him, rapier, scabbard, and all, and he gives me the stuck-in[2] with such a mortal motion, that it is inevitable;[3] and on the answer,[4] he pays you as surely as your feet hit the ground they step on: they say he has been fencer to the Sophy.

SIR ANDREW AGUECHEEK.

Pox on't, I'll not meddle with him.

SIR TOBY BELCH.

Ay, but he will not now be pacified: Fabian can scarce hold him yonder.

SIR ANDREW AGUECHEEK.

Plague on't, an I thought he had been valiant and so cunning in fence, I'ld have seen him damn'd ere I'ld have challenged him. Let him let the matter slip, and I'll give him my horse, gray Capulet.

SIR TOBY BELCH.

I'll make the motion:[5] stand here, make a good show on't: this shall end without the perdition of souls.[6]—[*aside*] Marry, I'll ride your horse as well as I ride you.

---

[1] firago: corruption of virago; possessing great strength and courage (a term usually applied to a violent woman). [2] stuck-in: thrust. [3] in/evitable: cannot be parried or stopped. [4] the answer: the return stroke. [5] make the motion: make the offer. [6] without the perdition of souls: without the death of either.

*Enter* FABIAN *and* VIOLA.

[*to* FABIAN] I have his horse to take up the quarrel:[1] I have persuaded him the youth's a devil.

FABIAN.

He is as horribly conceited of him;[2] and pants and looks pale, as if a bear were at his heels.

SIR TOBY BELCH [*to* VIOLA].

There's no remedy, sir; he will fight with you for's oath-sake: marry, he hath better bethought[3] him of his quarrel, and he finds that now scarce to be worth talking of: therefore draw, for the supportance of his vow; he protests he will not hurt you.

VIOLA [*aside*].

Pray God defend me! A little thing would make me tell them how much I lack of a man.

FABIAN.

Give ground, if you see him furious.

SIR TOBY BELCH.

Come, Sir Andrew, there's no remedy; the gentleman will, for his honour's sake, have one bout with you; he cannot by the duello[4] avoid it: but he has promised me, as he is a gentleman and a soldier, he will not hurt you. Come on, to't.

SIR ANDREW AGUECHEEK.

Pray God, he keep his oath!                    [*Draws.*

VIOLA.

I do assure you, 'tis against my will.            [*Draws.*

*Enter* ANTONIO.

ANTONIO.

Put up your sword. If this young gentleman
Have done offence, I take the fault on me:
If you offend him, I for him defy you.

---

[1] take up the quarrel: a gift of the horse to patch up the quarrel.
[2] conceited of him: has an extravagant idea of his fierce nature.
[3] bethought: second-thought.
[4] duello: the rules of dueling.

SIR TOBY BELCH.

You, sir! why, what are you?

ANTONIO [*drawing*].

One, sir, that for his love dares yet do more
Than you have heard him brag to you he will.

SIR TOBY BELCH.

Nay, if you be an undertaker,[1] I am for you.      [*Draws.*

FABIAN.

O good Sir Toby, hold! here come the officers.

SIR TOBY BELCH [*to* ANTONIO].

I'll be with you anon.

VIOLA [*to* SIR ANDREW].

Pray, sir, put your sword up, if you please.

SIR ANDREW AGUECHEEK.

Marry, will I, sir; and, for that I promised you, I'll be as good
as my word: he will bear you easily,[2] and reins well.

### Enter OFFICERS.

FIRST OFFICER.

This is the man; do thy office,[3]

SECOND OFFICER.

Antonio, I arrest thee at the suit of Count Orsino.

ANTONIO.

You do mistake me, sir.

FIRST OFFICER.

No, sir, no jot; I know your favour[4] well,
Though now you have no sea-cap on your head.—
Take him away: he knows I know him well.

ANTONIO.

I must obey. [*to* VIOLA] This comes with seeking you:
But there's no remedy; I shall answer it.

---

[1] be an undertaker: stand bond.
[2] he will bear you easily: Sir Andrew is speaking of his horse.
[3] office: duty.
[4] favour: face.

What will you do, now my necessity
Makes me to ask you for my purse? It grieves me
Much more for what I cannot do for you
Than what befalls myself. You stand amazed;
But be of comfort.

SECOND OFFICER.

Come sir, away.

ANTONIO.

I must entreat of you some of that money.

VIOLA.

What money, sir?
For the fair kindness you have show'd me here,
And, part, being prompted by your present trouble,
Out of my lean and low ability
I'll lend you something: my having is not much;
I'll make division of my present[1] with you:
Hold, there's half my coffer.[2]

ANTONIO.

Will you deny me now?
Is't possible that my deserts[3] to you
Can lack persuasion? Do not tempt my misery,
Lest that it make me so unsound[4] a man
As to upbraid you with those kindnesses
That I have done for you.

VIOLA.

I know of none;
Nor know I you by voice or any feature:
I hate ingratitude more in a man
Than lying, vainness, babbling, drunkenness,
Or any taint of vice whose strong corruption
Inhabits our frail blood.

ANTONIO.

O heavens themselves!

---

[1] my present: the money I have with me.
[2] coffer: hoard; funds.
[3] deserts: worthy deeds.
[4] unsound: unstable.

SECOND OFFICER.

Come, sir, I pray you, go.

ANTONIO.

Let me speak a little. This youth that you see here
I snatcht one half out of the jaws of death,
Relieved him with such sanctity of love,
And to his image, which methought did promise
Most venerable worth, did I devotion.

FIRST OFFICER.

What's that to us? The time goes by: away!

ANTONIO.

But, O, how vile an idol proves this god!
Thou hast, Sebastian, done good feature shame.[1]
In nature there's no blemish but the mind;
None can be call'd deform'd but the unkind:
Virtue is beauty: but the beauteous evil
Are empty trunks, o'erflourisht by the devil.[2]

FIRST OFFICER.

The man grows mad: away with him!—come, come, sir.

ANTONIO.

Lead me on.                    [*Exit with* OFFICERS.

VIOLA.

Methinks his words do from such passion fly,
That he believes himself: so do not I.
Prove true, imagination, O, prove true,
That I, dear brother, be now ta'en for you!

SIR TOBY BELCH.

Come hither, knight; come hither, Fabian: we'll whisper o'er
a couplet or two of most sage saws.[3]

VIOLA.

He named Sebastian: I my brother know
Yet living in my glass;[4] even such, and so,

---

[1] done good feature shame: belied your handsome appearance.
[2] beauteous evil/ Are empty trunks; o'erflourisht by the devil: evil
in fair guise is as empty treasure chests decorated by the devil to
fool the unwary.
[3] sage saws: wise sayings.
[4] living in my glass: looks as I do in my mirror.

In favour was my brother; and he went
Still in this fashion, colour, ornament,—
For him I imitate:[1] O, if it prove,
Tempests are kind, and salt waves fresh in love![2]    [*Exit.*

SIR TOBY BELCH.

A very dishonest paltry[3] boy, and more a coward than a hare:
his dishonesty appears in leaving his friend here in necessity,
**and** denying him; and for his cowardship, ask Fabian.

FABIAN.

A coward, a most devout coward, religious in it.

SIR ANDREW AGUECHEEK.

'Slid,[4] I'll after him again, and beat him.

SIR TOBY BELCH.

Do; cuff him soundly, but never draw thy sword.

SIR ANDREW AGUECHEEK.

An I do not,—    [*Exit.*

FABIAN.

Come, let's see the event.

SIR TOBY BELCH.

I dare lay any money 'twill be nothing yet.    [*Exeunt.*

---

[1] him I imitate: she patterns herself after him in dress and manners.
[2] salt waves fresh in love: salt water made sweet, or fresh, by love.
[3] paltry: worthless.
[4] 'Slid: by God's eyelid.

# Twelfth Night

## ACT 4

# ACT IV

SEBASTIAN now appears, mistaken for Cesario (Viola) first
by the Clown, and then by Sir Toby, Sir Andrew, and
Fabian. Sir Andrew attacks him and is surprised to find his
blow roundly returned. Sir Toby intervenes just as Olivia
enters and, making the same mistake as the others, addresses
Sebastian with words of endearment. Astonished but de-
lighted, he departs with her. Back at Olivia's house, Maria,
the Clown, and Sir Toby are baiting Malvolio in his dark
room. The Clown pretends to be a priest, Sir Topas, and
engages in mock-serious conversation with the steward, to the
great delight of Maria and Sir Toby. Sebastian, meanwhile,
completely captivated by Olivia's charms, has agreed to marry
her, Olivia, of course, believing him to be the page, Cesario.

## ACT IV. Scene I.

*Before* OLIVIA's *house.*

*Enter* SEBASTIAN *and* CLOWN.

CLOWN.

Will you make me believe that I am not sent for you?

SEBASTIAN.

Go to, go to, thou art a foolish fellow:
Let me be clear of thee.

CLOWN.

Well held out, i'faith! No, I do not know you; nor I am not
sent to you by my lady, to bid you come speak with her; nor
your name is not Master Cesario; nor this is not my nose
neither. Nothing that is so is so.

SEBASTIAN.

I prithee, vent[1] thy folly somewhere else;
Thou know'st not me.

CLOWN.

Vent my folly! he has heard that word of some great man,
and now applies it to a fool: vent my folly! I am afraid this
great lubber, the world, will prove a cockney.[2]—I prithee,
now, ungird thy strangeness,[3] and tell me what I shall vent
to my lady: shall I vent to her that thou art coming?

SEBASTIAN.

I prithee, foolish Greek,[4] depart from me:
There's money for thee: if you tarry longer,
I shall give worse payment.

CLOWN.

By my troth, thou hast an open hand.[5]—These wise men,
that give fools money, get themselves a good report after
fourteen years' purchase.[6]

*Enter* SIR ANDREW.

SIR ANDREW AGUECHEEK.

Now, sir, have I met you again? there's for you.

[*Striking* SEBASTIAN.

SEBASTIAN.

Why, there's for thee, and there, and there!

[*Beating* SIR ANDREW.

Are all the people mad?

*Enter* SIR TOBY *and* FABIAN.

SIR TOBY BELCH.

Hold, sir, or I'll throw your dagger o'er the house.

---

[1] vent: utter; express. [2] cockney: milksop; stupid person. [3] ungird
thy strangeness: drop your pretense of being a stranger. [4] foolish
Greek: strange speaking; Sebastian does not understand the clown's
language. [5] open hand: generous hand. [6] fourteen years' purchase:
a long, long time.

CLOWN.

This will I tell my lady straight:[1] I would not be in some of
your coats for twopence.                                    [Exit.

SIR TOBY BELCH.

Come on, sir; hold.

SIR ANDREW AGUECHEEK.

Nay, let him alone: I'll go another way to work with him;
I'll have an action of battery[2] against him, if there be any
law in Illyria: though I struck him first, yet it's no matter for
that.

SEBASTIAN.

Let go thy hand.

SIR TOBY BELCH.

Come, sir, I will not let you go. Come, my young soldier, put
up your iron:[3] you are well flesht;[4] come on.

SEBASTIAN.

I will be free from thee. What wouldst thou now? If thou
darest tempt me further, draw thy sword.            [Draws.

SIR TOBY BELCH.

What, what? Nay, then I must have an ounce or two of this
malapert[5] blood from you.                            [Draws.

*Enter* OLIVIA.

OLIVIA.

Hold, Toby; on thy life, I charge thee, hold!

SIR TOBY BELCH.

Madam!

OLIVIA.

Will it be ever thus? Ungracious wretch,
Fit for the mountains and the barbarous caves,

---

[1] straight: immediately.
[2] action of battery: assault.
[3] iron: sword.
[4] well flesht: inflamed with rage by a taste of blood.
[5] malapert: saucy.

Where manners ne'er were preacht! out of my sight!—
Be not offended, dear Cesario.—
Rudesby,[1] be gone!

     [*Exeunt* SIR TOBY, SIR ANDREW, *and* FABIAN.
     I prithee, gentle friend,
Let thy fair wisdom, not thy passion, sway
In this uncivil and unjust extent[2]
Against thy peace. Go with me to my house;
And hear thou there how many fruitless pranks
This ruffian hath botcht up, that thou thereby
Mayst smile at this: thou shalt not choose but go:
Do not deny. Beshrew[3] his soul for me,
He started one poor heart of mine in thee.

  SEBASTIAN.

What relish[4] is in this? how runs the stream?
Or I am mad, or else this is a dream:
Let fancy still my sense in Lethe[5] steep;
If it be thus to dream, still let me sleep!

  OLIVIA.

Nay, come, I prithee: would thou'ldst be ruled by me!

  SEBASTIAN.

Madam, I will.

  OLIVIA.

    O, say so, and so be!      [*Exeunt.*


## SCENE II.

### OLIVIA's *house.*


*Enter* MARIA *and* CLOWN.


 MARIA.

Nay, I prithee, put on this gown and this beard; make him

---

[1] **Rudesby**: an uncivil, quarrelsome person; madman.
[2] **extent**: behavior.
[3] **Beshrew**: a mild curse.
[4] **relish**: meaning.
[5] **Lethe**: oblivion: the river of forgetfulness in Hades.

believe thou art Sir Topas the curate: do it quickly; I'll call
Sir Toby the whilst.                                    [*Exit.*

    CLOWN.

Well, I'll put it on, and I will dissemble[1] myself in't; and I
would I were the first that ever dissembled in such a gown.
I am not tall enough to become the function well; nor lean
enough to be thought a good student: but to be said an
honest man and a good housekeeper, goes as fairly as to say
a careful man and a great scholar. The competitors[2] enter.

*Enter* SIR TOBY *and* MARIA.

    SIR TOBY BELCH.

Jove bless thee, master parson.

    CLOWN.

*Bonos dies,*[3] Sir Toby: for, as the old hermit of Prague, that
never saw pen and ink, very wittily said to a niece of King
Gorboduc,[4] 'That that is is;' so I, being master parson, am
master parson; for, what is that but that, and is but is?

    SIR TOBY BELCH.

To him, Sir Topas.

    CLOWN.

What, ho, I say,—peace in this prison!

    SIR TOBY BELCH.

The knave counterfeits well; a good knave.

    MALVOLIO [*within*].

Who calls there?

    CLOWN.

Sir Topas the curate, who comes to visit Malvolio the lunatic.

    MALVOLIO.

Sir Topas, Sir Topas, good Sir Topas, go to my lady.

---

[1] dissemble: disguise.
[2] competitors: confederates.
[3] *Bonos dies:* good day.
[4] hermit of/ Prague . . . /King Gorboduc: the Clown is talking in
a manner to sound impressive. "That that is is," etc., is foolery.

CLOWN.

Out, hyperbolical fiend! [1] how vexest thou this man! talkest
thou nothing but of ladies?

SIR TOBY BELCH.

Well said, master parson.

MALVOLIO.

Sir Topas, never was man thus wrong'd: good Sir Topas, do
not think I am mad: they have laid me here in hideous
darkness.

CLOWN.

Fie, thou dishonest Satan! I call thee by the most modest
terms; for I am one of those gentle ones that will use the
devil himself with courtesy: say'st thou that house is dark?

MALVOLIO.

As hell, Sir Topas.

CLOWN.

Why, it hath bay windows transparent as barricadoes,[2] and
the clearstories toward the south-north[3] are as lustrous as
ebony; and yet complainest thou of obstruction?

MALVOLIO.

I am not mad, Sir Topas: I say to you, this house is dark.

CLOWN.

Madman, thou errest: I say, there is no darkness but ignorance; in which thou art more puzzled than the Egyptians in
their fog.

MALVOLIO.

I say, this house is as dark as ignorance, though ignorance

---

[1] hyberbolical fiend: fiendishness beyond all limits.
[2] barricadoes: barricades.
[3] clearstories toward the south-north: nonsensical talk; clearstories are clerestories (gallery windows).

were as dark as hell; and I say, there was never man thus abused. I am no more mad than you are: make the trial of it in any constant[1] question.

CLOWN.

What is the opinion of Pythagoras[2] concerning wildfowl?

MALVOLIO.

That the soul of our grandam might haply[3] inhabit a bird.

CLOWN.

What think'st thou of his opinion?

MALVOLIO.

I think nobly of the soul, and no way approve his opinion.

CLOWN.

Fare thee well. Remain thou still in darkness: thou shalt hold the opinion of Pythagoras ere I will allow of thy wits; and fear to kill a woodcock, lest thou dispossess the soul of thy grandam. Fare thee well.

MALVOLIO.

Sir Topas, Sir Topas,—

SIR TOBY BELCH.

My most exquisite Sir Topas!

CLOWN.

Nay, I am for all waters.

MARIA.

Thou mightst have done this without thy beard and gown: he sees thee not.

SIR TOBY BELCH.

To him in thine own voice, and bring me word how thou find'st him: I would we were well rid of this knavery. If he

---

[1] constant: rational.
[2] Pythagoras: a Greek philosopher.
[3] haply: by chance.

may be conveniently deliver'd,[1] I would he were; for I am now so far in offence with my niece, that I cannot pursue with any safety this sport to the upshot.[2] Come by and by to my chamber.           [*Exeunt* SIR TOBY *and* MARIA.

CLOWN [*singing*].
> Hey, Robin, jolly Robin,
> > Tell me how thy lady does.

MALVOLIO.

Fool,—

CLOWN.

'My lady is unkind, perdy.' [3]

MALVOLIO.

Fool,—

CLOWN.

'Alas, why is she so?'

MALVOLIO.

Fool, I say,—

CLOWN.

'She loves another'—Who calls, ha?

MALVOLIO.

Good fool, as ever thou wilt deserve well at my hand, help me to a candle, and pen, ink, and paper: as I am a gentleman, I will live to be thankful to thee for't.

CLOWN.

Master Malvolio!

MALVOLIO.

Ay, good fool.

CLOWN.

Alas, sir, how fell you besides your five wits? [4]

MALVOLIO.

Fool, there was never man so notoriously abused: I am as well in my wits, fool, as thou art.

---

[1] deliver'd: freed.
[2] upshot: conclusion.
[3] perdy: a mild oath; corruption of *par dieu*.
[4] how fell you besides your five wits: how did you lose your senses?

CLOWN.

But as well? then you are mad indeed, if you be no better in
your wits than a fool.

MALVOLIO.

They have here propertied me;[1] keep me in darkness, send
ministers to me, asses, and do all they can to face me out of
my wits.

CLOWN.

Advise[2] you what you say; the minister is here.—Malvolio,
Malvolio, thy wits the heavens restore! endeavour thyself to
sleep, and leave thy vain bibble-babble.

MALVOLIO.

Sir Topas,—

CLOWN.

Maintain no words with him, good fellow.—Who, I, sir? not
I, sir. God b'wi'you, good Sir Topas!—Marry, amen.—I will,
sir, I will.

MALVOLIO.

Fool, fool, fool, I say,—

CLOWN.

Alas, sir, be patient. What say you, sir? I am shent[3] for speaking to you.

MALVOLIO.

Good fool, help me to some light and some paper: I tell thee,
I am as well in my wits as any man in Illyria.

CLOWN.

Well-a-day, that you were, sir!

MALVOLIO.

By this hand, I am. Good fool, some ink, paper, and light;

---

[1] propertied me: taken possession of me.
[2] advise: be careful.
[3] shent: shamed.

and convey what I will set down to my lady: it shall advantage thee more than ever the bearing of letter did.

CLOWN.

I will help you to't. But tell me true, are you not mad indeed? or do you but counterfeit?

MALVOLIO.

Believe me, I am not; I tell thee true.

CLOWN.

Nay, I'll ne'er believe a madman till I see his brains. I will fetch you light, and paper, and ink.

MALVOLIO.

Fool, I'll requite it in the highest degree: I prithee, be gone.

CLOWN [singing].

　　　I am gone, sir,
　　　　And anon, sir,
　　　I'll be with you again,
　　　　In a trice,
　　　　Like to the old Vice,
　　　Your need to sustain;
　　　Who, with dagger of lath,
　　　In his rage and his wrath,
　　　　Cries, ah, ha! to the devil:
　　　Like a mad lad,
　　　Pare thy nails, dad;
　　　　Adieu, goodman devil.　　　　　[Exit.

## SCENE III.

### OLIVIA's garden.

#### Enter SEBASTIAN.

SEBASTIAN.

This is the air; that is the glorious sun;
This pearl she gave me, I do feel't and see't:

And though 'tis wonder that enwraps me thus,
Yet 'tis not madness. Where's Antonio, then?
I could not find him at the Elephant:[1]
Yet there he was; and there I found this credit,[2]
That he did range the town to seek me out.
His counsel now might do me golden service;
For though my soul disputes well with my sense,
That this may be some error, but no madness,
Yet doth this accident and flood of fortune
So far exceed all instance,[3] all discourse,[4]
That I am ready to distrust mine eyes,
And wrangle with my reason, that persuades me
To any other trust but that I am mad
Or else the lady's mad; yet, if 'twere so,
She could not sway her house, command her followers,
Take and give back affairs, and their dispatch,
With such a smooth, discreet, and stable bearing,
As I perceive she does: there's something in't
That is deceivable. But here the lady comes.

*Enter* OLIVIA *and a* PRIEST.

OLIVIA.

Blame not this haste of mine. If you mean well,
Now go with me and with his holy man
Into the chantry[5] by: there, before him,
And underneath that consecrated roof,
Plight me the full assurance of your faith;
That my most jealous[6] and too doubtful soul
May live at peace: he shall conceal it,
Whiles you are willing it shall come to note,
What time we will our celebration keep
According to my birth.[7]—What do you say?

---

[1] Elephant: an inn. [2] credit: intelligence; report. [3] instance: precedent. [4] discourse: reasoning. [5] chantry: chapel. [6] jealous: distrustful. [7] birth: rank.

SEBASTIAN.

I'll follow this good man, and go with you;
And, having sworn truth, ever will be true.

OLIVIA.

Then lead the way, good father; and heavens so shine,
That they may fairly note this act of mine!　　　　[*Exeunt.*

# Twelfth Night

## ACT 5

# ACT V

THE DUKE, with Viola and other attendants, arrives in front
of Olivia's house. Antonio is brought in by the officers, still
demanding his purse from the supposed Sebastian. The Duke
recognizes his old enemy, and Antonio explains why he has
ventured to come where he is unwelcome: his affection for
the youth whose life he saved and who now disclaims acquaintance with him. At this point, Olivia enters addressing
Viola as her husband Cesario, and when Viola denies the fact
Olivia calls in a priest to confirm it. The Duke now accuses
Cesario of deceit, and Viola is completely at a loss to explain
the confused situation. Confusion is added to confusion when
Sir Andrew and Sir Toby appear declaring that they have
been attacked and wounded by Cesario. But all is resolved
when Sebastian himself arrives. Cesario's true identity is revealed; brother and sister are joyfully reunited; the Duke
gladly accepts Viola as his wife; and Olivia and Sebastian are
happy that their betrothal is true. Sir Toby, too, is to be
wedded to Maria. Malvolio appears, released now from his
prison and breathing vengeance on his tormentors. But he
soon leaves, permitting the Clown to end the play with a
song.

## ACT V.  SCENE I.

*Before* OLIVIA'*s house.*

*Enter* CLOWN *and* FABIAN.

FABIAN.
Now, as thou lovest me, let me see his letter.

CLOWN.
Good Master Fabian, grant me another request.

FABIAN.
Any thing.

CLOWN.
Do not desire to see this letter.

FABIAN.
This is, to give a dog, and in recompense desire my dog again.

*Enter* DUKE, VIOLA, CURIO, *and* ATTENDANTS.

DUKE OF ILLYRIA.
Belong you to the Lady Olivia, friends?

CLOWN.
Ay, sir; we are some of her trappings.[1]

DUKE OF ILLYRIA.
I know thee well: how dost thou, my good fellow?

---

[1] **trappings:** ornamental equipment.

CLOWN.

Truly, sir, the better for my foes, and the worse for my friends.

DUKE OF ILLYRIA.

Just the contrary; the better for thy friends.

CLOWN.

No, sir, the worse.

DUKE OF ILLYRIA.

How can that be?

CLOWN.

Marry, sir, they praise me, and make an ass of me; now my foes tell me plainly I am an ass: so that by my foes, sir, I profit in the knowledge of myself; and by my friends I am abused:[1] so that, conclusions to be as kisses, if your four negatives make your two affirmatives, why, then, the worse for my friends, and the better for my foes.

DUKE OF ILLYRIA.

Why, this is excellent.

CLOWN.

By my troth, sir, no; though it please you to be one of my friends.

DUKE OF ILLYRIA.

Thou shalt not be the worse for me: there's gold.

                             [*Gives money.*

CLOWN.

But that it would be double-dealing, sir, I would you could make it another.

DUKE OF ILLYRIA.

O, you give me ill counsel.

CLOWN.

Put your grace in your pocket, sir, for this once, and let your flesh and blood obey it.

---

[1] abused: deceived.

DUKE OF ILLYRIA.

Well, I will be so much a sinner to be a double-dealer: there's another.     [*Gives money.*

CLOWN.

*Primo, secundo, tertio,* is a good play; and the old saying is, the third pays for all: the *triplex,* sir, is a good tripping measure; or the bells of Saint Bennet, sir, may put you in mind,— one, two, three.

DUKE OF ILLYRIA.

You can fool no more money out of me at this throw: if you will let your lady know I am here to speak with her, and bring her along with you, it may awake my bounty further.

CLOWN.

Marry, sir, lullaby to your bounty till I come again. I go, sir; but I would not have you to think that my desire of having is the sin of covetousness: but, as you say, sir, let your bounty take a nap, I will awake it anon.     [*Exit.*

VIOLA.

Here comes the man, sir, that did rescue me.

*Enter* OFFICERS, *with* ANTONIO.

DUKE OF ILLYRIA.

That face of his I do remember well;
Yet, when I saw it last, it was besmear'd
As black as Vulcan[1] in the smoke of war:
A bawbling[2] vessel was he captain of,
For shallow draught and bulk unprizable;
With which such scatheful[3] grapple did he make
With the most noble bottom[4] of our fleet,
That very envy and the tongue of loss[5]
Cried fame and honour on him.—What's the matter?

---

[1] Vulcan: ancient Roman God of destructive fire and metalworking.
[2] bawbling: trifling (baubling).
[3] scatheful: harmful.
[4] bottom: ship.
[5] envy and the tongue of loss: his enemies who had lost.

**FIRST OFFICER.**

Orsino, this is that Antonio
That took the Phœnix[1] and her fraught[2] from Candy;[3]
And this is he that did the Tiger[4] board,
When your young nephew Titus lost his leg:
Here in the streets, desperate of shame and state,
In private brabble[5] did we apprehend him.

**VIOLA.**

He did me kindness, sir; drew on my side;
But, in conclusion, put strange speech upon me,—
I know not what 'twas but distraction.

**DUKE OF ILLYRIA.**

Notable pirate! thou salt-water thief!
What foolish boldness brought thee to their mercies,
Whom thou, in terms so bloody and so dear,
Hast made thine enemies?

**ANTONIO.**

                 Orsino, noble sir,
Be pleased that I shake off these names you give me:
Antonio never yet was thief or pirate,
Though, I confess, on base and ground enough,[6]
Orsino's enemy. A witchcraft drew me hither:
That most ingrateful boy there by your side,
From the rude sea's enraged and foamy mouth
Did I redeem; a wreck past hope he was:
His life I gave him, and did thereto add
My love, without retention or restraint,
All his in dedication; for his sake
Did I expose myself, pure for his love,

---

[1] **Phœnix:** a ship.
[2] **fraught:** freight; cargo.
[3] **Candy:** Candia, a small island off the coast of Crete.
[4] **Tiger:** a ship.
[5] **brabble:** brawl.
[6] **ground enough:** good and sufficient reason.

Into the danger of this adverse[1] town;
Drew to defend him when he was beset:
Where being apprehended, his false cunning,
Not meaning to partake with me in danger,
Taught him to face me out of his acquaintance,[2]
And grew a twenty-years-removed thing
While one would wink; denied me mine own purse,
Which I had recommended to[3] his use
Not half an hour before.

VIOLA.
                              How can this be?

DUKE OF ILLYRIA.
When came he to this town?

ANTONIO.
To-day, my lord: and for three months before—
No interim, not a minute's vacancy—
Both day and night did we keep company.

DUKE OF ILLYRIA.
Here comes the countess: now heaven walks on earth.—
But for thee, fellow; fellow, thy words are madness:
Three months this youth hath tended upon me;
But more of that anon. Take him aside.

*Enter* OLIVIA *and* ATTENDANTS.

OLIVIA.
What would my lord, but that he may not have,
Wherein Olivia may seem serviceable?—
Cesario, you do not keep promise with me.

VIOLA.
Madam!

DUKE OF ILLYRIA.
Gracious Olivia,—

---

[1] adverse: hostile.
[2] face me out of his acquaintance: denied knowing me.
[3] recommended to: offered for.

OLIVIA.

What do you say, Cesario? Good my lord,—

VIOLA.

My lord would speak; my duty hushes me.

OLIVIA.

If it be aught to the old tune, my lord,
It is as fat and fulsome to mine ear
As howling after music.

DUKE OF ILLYRIA.

                         Still so cruel?

OLIVIA.

Still so constant, lord.

DUKE OF ILLYRIA.

What, to perverseness? you uncivil lady,
To whose ingrate and unauspicious altars
My soul the faithfull'st offerings hath breathed out
That e'er devotion tender'd! What shall I do?

OLIVIA.

Even what it please my lord, that shall become him.

DUKE OF ILLYRIA.

Why should I not, had I the heart to do it,
Like to th'Egyptian thief at point of death,
Kill what I love? a savage jealousy
That sometimes savours nobly.[1]—But hear me this:
Since you to non-regardance cast my faith,[2]
And that I partly know the instrument[3]
That screws[4] me from my true place in your favour,
Live you, the marble-breasted tyrant, still;
But this your minion,[5] whom I know you love,
And whom, by heaven I swear, I tender[6] dearly,

---

[1] savours nobly: seems touched with nobility.
[2] to non-regardance cast my faith: reject my love.
[3] instrument: his rival.
[4] screws: removes.
[5] minion: favorite; darling.
[6] tender: regard.

Him will I tear out of that cruel eye,[1]
Where he sits crowned in his master's spite.—
Come, boy, with me; my thoughts are ripe in mischief:
I'll sacrifice the lamb that I do love,
To spite a raven's heart within a dove.

> VIOLA.

And I, most jocund,[2] apt, and willingly,
To do you rest, a thousand deaths would die.

> OLIVIA.

Where goes Cesario?

> VIOLA.

                    After him I love
More than I love these eyes, more than my life,
More, by all mores, than e'er I shall love wife.
If I do feign,[3] you witnesses above
Punish my life for tainting of my love!

> OLIVIA.

Ay me, detested! how am I beguiled![4]

> VIOLA.

Who does beguile you? who does do you wrong?

> OLIVIA.

Hast thou forgot thyself? is it so long?
Call forth the holy father.                    [*Exit an* ATTENDANT

> DUKE OF ILLYRIA.

                    Come, away!          [*to* VIOLA

> OLIVIA.

Whither, my lord?—Cesario, husband, stay.

> DUKE OF ILLYRIA.

Husband!

> OLIVIA.

          Ay, husband: can he that deny?

---

[1] cruel eye: Olivia's regard.
[2] jocund: cheerfully.
[3] feign: lie.
[4] Ay me, detested! how am I beguiled!: Alas, I am despised, deceived!

DUKE OF ILLYRIA.

Her husband, sirrah!

VIOLA.

No, my lord, not I.

OLIVIA.

Alas, it is the baseness of thy fear
That makes thee strangle thy propriety:[1]
Fear not, Cesario; take thy fortunes up;[2]
Be that thou know'st thou art,[3] and then thou art
As great as that thou fear'st.[4]

*Enter* ATTENDANT, *with* PRIEST.

O, welcome, father!
Father, I charge thee, by thy reverence,
Here to unfold—though lately we intended
To keep in darkness what occasion now
Reveals before 'tis ripe—what thou dost know
Hath newly past between this youth and me.

PRIEST.

A contract of eternal bond of love,
Confirm'd by mutual joinder of your hands,
Attested by the holy close of lips,[5]
Strengthen'd by interchangement of your rings;
And all the ceremony of this compact
Seal'd in my function,[6] by my testimony:
Since when, my watch hath told me, toward my grave
I have travell'd but two hours.

DUKE OF ILLYRIA.

O thou dissembling cub! what wilt thou be
When time hath sow'd a grizzle on thy case?[7]
Or will not else thy craft[8] so quickly grow,
That thine own trip[9] shall be thine overthrow?
Farewell, and take her; but direct thy feet

---

[1] strangle thy propriety: lose sight of your true worth. [2] take thy fortunes up: welcome your good fortune. [3] that thou know'st thou art: Olivia's husband. [4] that thou fear'st: Orsini. [5] holy close of lips: wedding kiss. [6] Seal'd in my function: solemnized by my priestly office. [7] sow'd a grizzle on thy case: turned the hair on your head gray, or gray-black, a mark of age. [8] craft: deceit. [9] trip: slip; mistake.

Where thou and I henceforth may never meet.

VIOLA.

My lord, I do protest,—

OLIVIA.

O, do not swear!

Hold little faith, though thou hast too much fear.

*Enter* SIR ANDREW.

SIR ANDREW AGUECHEEK.

For the love of God, a surgeon! send one presently to Sir Toby.

OLIVIA.

What's the matter?

SIR ANDREW AGUECHEEK.

'Has broke my head across, and has given Sir Toby a bloody coxcomb[1] too: for the love of God, your help! I had rather than forty pound I were at home.

OLIVIA.

Who has done this, Sir Andrew?

SIR ANDREW AGUECHEEK.

The count's gentleman, one Cesario: we took him for a coward, but he's the very devil incardinate.[2]

DUKE OF ILLYRIA.

My gentleman Cesario?

SIR ANDREW AGUECHEEK.

'Od's lifelings,[3] here he is!—You broke my head for nothing; and that that I did, I was set on to do't by Sir Toby.

VIOLA.

Why do you speak to me? I never hurt you:
You drew your sword upon me without cause;
But I bespake you fair, and hurt you not.

SIR ANDREW AGUECHEEK.

If a bloody coxcomb be a hurt, you have hurt me: I think

---

[1] coxcomb: head.
[2] incardinate: corruption of "incarnate"; the devil in the flesh.
[3] 'Od's lifelings: by God's life.

you set nothing by a bloody coxcomb.—Here comes Sir Toby halting;[1] you shall hear more: but if he had not been in drink, he would have tickled you othergates[2] than he did.

*Enter* SIR TOBY *and* CLOWN.

DUKE OF ILLYRIA.

How now, gentleman! how is't with you?

SIR TOBY BELCH.

That's all one: has hurt me, and there's the end on't.—Sot, didst see Dick surgeon, sot?

CLOWN.

O, he's drunk, Sir Toby, an hour agone; his eyes were set[3] at eight i'th'morning.

SIR TOBY BELCH.

Then he's a rogue and a passy-measures pavin:[4] I hate a drunken rogue.

OLIVIA.

Away with him! Who hath made this havoc with them?

SIR ANDREW AGUECHEEK.

I'll help you, Sir Toby, because we'll be drest[5] together.

SIR TOBY BELCH.

Will you help? an ass-head and a coxcomb and a knave, a thin-faced knave, a gull? [6]

OLIVIA.

Get him to bed, and let his hurt be lookt to.

[*Exeunt* CLOWN, FABIAN, SIR TOBY, *and* SIR ANDREW.

*Enter* SEBASTIAN.

SEBASTIAN.

I am sorry, madam, I have hurt your kinsman;
But, had it been the brother of my blood,

---

[1] halting: limping.
[2] othergates: in other ways.
[3] set: glazed.
[4] passy-measures pavin: an obscure phrase.
[5] drest: bandaged by the surgeon.
[6] gull: fool.

I must have done no less with wit[1] and safety.
You throw a strange regard [2] upon me, and by that
I do perceive it hath offended you:
Pardon me, sweet one, even for the vows
We made each other but so late ago.

DUKE OF ILLYRIA.

One face, one voice, one habit,[3] and two persons,—
A natural perspective, that is and is not!

SEBASTIAN.

Antonio, O my dear Antonio!
How have the hours rackt and tortured me,
Since I have lost thee!

ANTONIO.

Sebastian are you?

SEBASTIAN.

Fear'st thou that, Antonio?

ANTONIO.

How have you made division of yourself?
An apple, cleft in two, is not more twin
Than these two creatures. Which is Sebastian?

OLIVIA.

Most wonderful!

SEBASTIAN.

Do I stand there? I never had a brother;
Nor can there be that deity in my nature,
Of here and every where.[4] I had a sister,
Whom the blind waves and surges have devour'd.—
Of charity, what kin are you to me?                    [to VIOLA.
What countryman? what name? what parentage?

VIOLA.

Of Messaline: Sebastian was my father;
Such a Sebastian was my brother too,

---

[1] wit: reason.
[2] throw a strange regard: look at strangely.
[3] habit: costume.
[4] deity in my nature/ Of here and every where: have God's power
of being everywhere at the same time.

So went he suited [1] to his watery tomb:
If spirits can assume both form and suit,
You come to fright us.

SEBASTIAN.

A spirit I am indeed;
But am in that dimension grossly clad,
Which from the womb I did participate.[2]
Were you a woman, as the rest goes even,
I should my tears let fall upon your cheek,
And say, 'Thrice-welcome, drowned Viola!'

VIOLA.

My father had a mole upon his brow,—

SEBASTIAN.

And so had mine.

VIOLA.

And died that day when Viola from her birth
Had number'd thirteen years.

SEBASTIAN.

O, that record is lively in my soul!
He finished, indeed, his mortal act
That day that made my sister thirteen years.

VIOLA.

If nothing lets to make us happy both
But this my masculine usurpt[3] attire,
Do not embrace me till each circumstance
Of place, time, fortune, do cohere and jump,[4]
That I am Viola: which to confirm,
I'll bring you to a captain in this town,
Where lie my maiden weeds;[5] by whose gentle help
I was preserved to serve this noble count.
All the occurrence of my fortune since
Hath been between this lady and this lord.

---

[1] suited: clad.
[2] But am in that dimension grossly clad/ Which from the womb I did participate: the physical form which he has had since birth.
[3] usurpt: assumed.
[4] cohere and jump: agree, and arrive at the conclusion.
[5] maiden weeds: her own clothes.

SEBASTIAN [to OLIVIA].

So comes it, lady, you have been mistook:
But nature to her bias drew[1] in that.
You would have been contracted to a maid;
Nor are you therein, by my life, deceived,—
You are betrothed both to a maid and man.

DUKE OF ILLYRIA.

Be not amazed; right noble is his blood.—
If this be so, as yet the glass seems true,[2]
I shall have share in this most happy wrack.—
[to VIOLA] Boy, thou hast said to me a thousand times
Thou never shouldst love woman like to me.

VIOLA.

And all those sayings will I over-swear;
And all those swearings keep as true in soul
As doth that orbed continent[3] the fire
That severs day from night.

DUKE OF ILLYRIA.

                              Give me thy hand;
And let me see thee in thy woman's weeds.

VIOLA.

The captain that did bring me first on shore
Hath my maid's garments: he, upon some action,
Is now in durance,[4] at Malvolio's suit,
A gentleman and follower of my lady's.

OLIVIA.

He shall enlarge him:[5]—fetch Malvolio hither:—
And yet, alas, now I remember me,
They say, poor gentleman, he's much distract.

*Enter* CLOWN *with a letter, and* FABIAN.

A most extracting[6] frenzy of mine own
From my remembrance clearly banish his.—

---

[1] **to her bias drew:** followed her natural inclination; bias—the
weighted side of a bowl in lawn bowling. [2] **glass seems true:** there's
no distortion. [3] **orbed continent:** the sun. [4] **in durance:** imprisoned.
[5] **enlarge him:** free him. [6] **extracting:** distracting.

How does he, sirrah?

CLOWN.

Truly, madam, he holds Beelzebub[1] at the stave's end as well
as a man in his case may do: has here writ a letter to you;
I should have given't you to-day morning, but as a madman's
epistles are no gospels, so it skills[2] not much when they are
deliver'd.

OLIVIA.

Open't, and read it.

CLOWN.

Look, then, to be well edified when the fool delivers the madman. [reads] By the Lord, madam,—

OLIVIA.

How now! art thou mad?

CLOWN.

No, madam, I do but read madness: an your ladyship will
have it as it ought to be, you must allow vox.[3]

OLIVIA.

Prithee, read i'thy right wits.

CLOWN.

So I do, madonna; but to read his right wits is to read thus:
therefore perpend,[4] my princess, and give ear.

OLIVIA.

Read it you, sirrah.             [to FABIAN.

FABIAN [reads].

By the Lord, madam, you wrong me, and the world shall
know it: though you have put me into darkness, and given
your drunken cousin rule over me, yet have I the benefit of

---

[1] Beelzebub: "prince of demons"—Matthew 12:24; the Devil.
[2] skills: matters.
[3] vox: voice.
[4] perpend: reflect; consider; be attentive.

my senses as well as your ladyship. I have your own letter that induced me to the semblance I put on; with the which I doubt not but to do myself much right, or you much shame. Think of me as you please. I leave my duty a little unthought of, and speak out of my injury.

THE MADLY-USED MALVOLIO.

OLIVIA.

Did he write this?

CLOWN.

Ay, madam.

DUKE OF ILLYRIA.

This savours not much of distraction.

OLIVIA.

See him deliver'd,[1] Fabian; bring him hither.    [Exit FABIAN.
My lord, so please you, these things further thought on,
To think me as well a sister as a wife,[2]
One day shall crown th'alliance on't, so please you,
Here at my house, and at my proper cost.[3]

DUKE OF ILLYRIA.

Madam, I am most apt t'embrace your offer.—
[to VIOLA] Your master quits[4] you; and, for your service done
  him,
So much against the mettle of your sex,
So far beneath your soft and tender breeding,
And since you call'd me master for so long,
Here is my hand: you shall from this time be
Your master's mistress.

OLIVIA.

                    A sister!—you are she.

---

[1] deliver'd: set free.
[2] To think me as well a sister as a wife: to think of me as a sister-in-law, instead of a wife.
[3] at my proper cost: at my expense.
[4] quits: discharges.

*Enter* FABIAN, *with* MALVOLIO.

DUKE OF ILLYRIA.

Is this the madman?

OLIVIA.

                Ay, my lord, this same.—

How now, Malvolio!

MALVOLIO.

                Madam, you have done me wrong,

Notorious wrong.

OLIVIA.

            Have I, Malvolio? no.

MALVOLIO.

Lady, you have. Pray you, peruse that letter:
You must not now deny it is your hand,—
Write from it, if you can, in hand or phrase;
Or say 'tis not your seal, not your invention:
You can say none of this: well, grant it, then,
And tell me, in the modesty of honour,
Why you have given me such clear lights[1] of favour,
Bade me come smiling and cross-garter'd to you.
To put on yellow stockings, and to frown
Upon Sir Toby and the lighter[2] people;
And, acting this in an obedient hope,
Why have you suffer'd me to be imprison'd,
Kept in a dark house, visited by the priest,
And made the most notorious geck and gull [3]
That e'er invention play'd on? tell me why.

OLIVIA.

Alas, Malvolio, this is not my writing,
Though, I confess, much like the character:[4]
But, out of question, 'tis Maria's hand.
And now I do bethink me, it was she

---

[1] **clear lights:** open signs.
[2] **lighter:** lesser.
[3] **geck and gull:** dupe and fool.
[4] **character:** handwriting.

First told me thou wast mad: thou camest in smiling,
And in such forms which here were presupposed
Upon thee in the letter. Prithee, be content:
This practice hath most shrewdly past upon thee;
But, when we know the grounds and authors of it,
Thou shalt be both the plaintiff and the judge
Of thine own cause.

    FABIAN.

                Good madam, hear me speak:
And let no quarrel nor no brawl to come
Taint the condition of this present hour,
Which I have wonder'd at. In hope it shall not,
Most freely I confess, myself and Toby
Set this device against Malvolio here,
Upon some stubborn and uncourteous parts[1]
We had conceived in him: Maria writ
The letter at Sir Toby's great importance;
In recompense whereof he hath married her.
How with a sportful malice[2] it was follow'd,
May rather pluck on[3] laughter than revenge;
If that the injuries be justly weigh'd
That have on both sides past.

    OLIVIA.

Alas, poor fool, how have they baffled thee!

    CLOWN.

Why, 'some are born great, some achieve greatness, and some
have greatness thrown upon them.' I was one, sir, in this
interlude,—one Sir Topas, sir; but that's all one.—'By the
Lord, fool, I am not mad;'—but do you remember? 'Madam,

---

[1] stubborn and uncourteous parts: intractable and ungracious characteristics.
[2] sportful malice: playful meanness.
[3] pluck on: excite.

why laugh you at such a barren rascal? an you smile not, he's
gagg'd:' and thus the whirligig of time brings in his revenges.

MALVOLIO.

I'll be revenged on the whole pack of you.         [*Exit.*

OLIVIA.

He hath been most notoriously abused.[1]

DUKE OF ILLYRIA.

Pursue him, and entreat him to a peace:—
He hath not told us of the captain yet:
When that is known, and golden time convents,[2]
A solemn combination shall be made
Of our dear souls. Meantime, sweet sister,
We will not part from hence.—Cesario, come;
For so you shall be, while you are a man;
But when in other habits you are seen,
Orsino's mistress and his fancy's[3] queen.

                     [*Exeunt all, except* CLOWN.

    CLOWN [*sings*].

       When that I was and a little tiny boy,      18½ px
          With hey, ho, the wind and the rain,
       A foolish thing was but a toy,
          For the rain it raineth every day.
       But when I came to man's estate,
          With hey, ho, the wind and the rain,
       'Gainst knaves and thieves men shut their gate,
          For the rain it raineth every day.
       But when I came, alas! to wive,
          With hey, ho, the wind and the rain,
       By swaggering could I never thrive,
          For the rain it raineth every day.

---

[1] **notoriously abused**: widely wronged.
[2] **convents**: is convenient.
[3] **fancy's**: love's.

But when I came unto my beds,
  With hey, ho, the wind and the rain,
With toss-pots still had drunken heads,
  For the rain it raineth every day.
A great while ago the world begun,
  With hey, ho, the wind and the rain:—
But that's all one, our play is done,
  And we'll strive to please you every day.          [*Exit.*